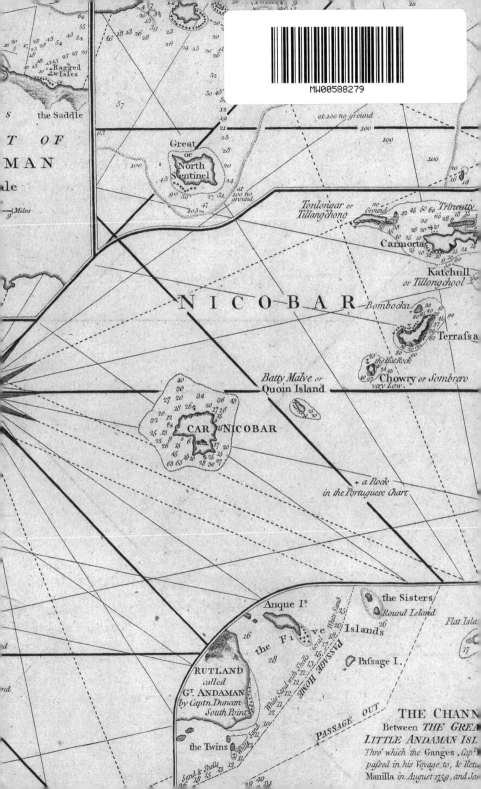

The Last Island

ALSO BY ADAM GOODHEART

1861:
The Civil War Awakening

The Last Island

Discovery, Defiance, and
the Most Elusive Tribe on Earth

ADAM GOODHEART

GODINE | BOSTON | 2023

Published in 2023 by
GODINE
Boston, Massachusetts

FRONTISPIECE: *Unknown young Andamanese photographed by
Maurice Vidal Portman, c. 1890s, from his private albums in Calcutta.
Courtesy of the Anthropological Survey of India.*

ENDPAPERS: *"A New Chart of the Andaman and Nicobar Islands, with
Adjacent Islands," 1799 (detail). From the author's collection.*

LIBRARY OF CONGRESS CATALOGING-IN-PUBLICATION DATA
Names: Goodheart, Adam, author.
Title: The last island : discovery, defiance, and the most elusive tribe on
earth / Adam Goodheart.
Description: Boston : Godine, 2023.
Identifiers: LCCN 2023002219 (print) | LCCN 2023002220 (ebook) |
ISBN 9781567926828 (hardcover) | ISBN 9781567926842 (ebook)
Subjects: LCSH: Sentinelese (Indic people) | Andaman Islands
(India)--History. | Andaman Islands (India)--Foreign relations.
Classification: LCC DS432.S42 G66 2023 (print) | LCC DS432.S42
(ebook) | DDC 305.8959--dc23/eng/20230124
LC record available at https://lccn.loc.gov/2023002219
LC ebook record available at https://lccn.loc.gov/2023002220

First Printing, 2023
Printed in the United States of America

For Avery, Logan, and Ben

and with gratitude to Trevor and Dana

The lumps of white coral shone round the dark mound like a chaplet of bleached skulls, and everything around was so quiet that when I stood still all sound and all movement in the world seemed to come to an end. It was a great peace, as if the earth had been one grave, and for a time I stood there thinking mostly of the living who, buried in remote places out of the knowledge of mankind, still are fated to share in its tragic or grotesque miseries. In its noble struggles too— who knows? The human heart is vast enough to contain all the world. It is valiant enough to bear the burden, but where is the courage that would cast it off?

—JOSEPH CONRAD, *Lord Jim* (1900)

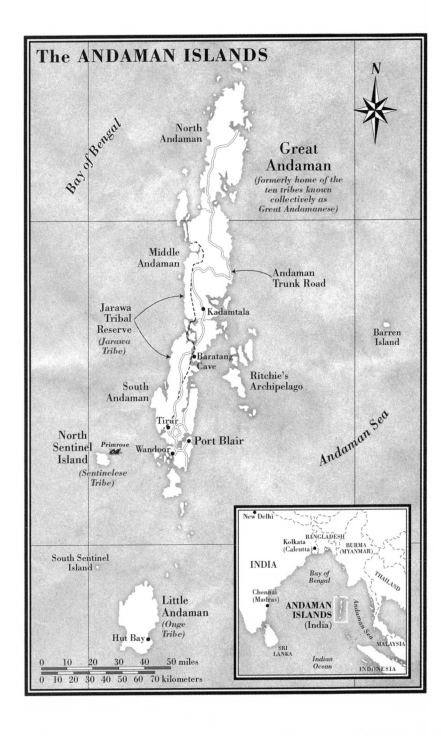

The ANDAMAN ISLANDS

N

Bay of Bengal

North Andaman

Great Andaman
(formerly home of the ten tribes known collectively as Great Andamanese)

Middle Andaman

Andaman Trunk Road

Jarawa Tribal Reserve *(Jarawa Tribe)*

Kadamtala

Barren Island

Baratang Cave

Ritchie's Archipelago

South Andaman

Tirur

North Sentinel Island *(Sentinelese Tribe)*

Primrose

Wandoor

Port Blair

Andaman Sea

South Sentinel Island

Little Andaman *(Onge Tribe)*

Hut Bay

| 0 | 10 | 20 | 30 | 40 | 50 miles |
| 0 | 10 | 20 | 30 | 40 | 50 | 60 | 70 kilometers |

New Delhi

BANGLADESH

Kolkata (Calcutta)

BURMA (MYANMAR)

INDIA

Bay of Bengal

THAILAND

Chennai (Madras)

ANDAMAN ISLANDS (India)

Andaman Sea

MALAYSIA

SRI LANKA

Indian Ocean

INDONESIA

CONTENTS

I

Isles of the Blessed

The wreck of the Primrose, *1981*

And when he heard the sailors' tales, he was seized with a marvelous desire to dwell in those Isles of the Blessed—to live quietly there, freed from kings and ceaseless wars.

—PLUTARCH, *Life of Sertorius* (c. 100 A.D.)

I looked about, and there was none to help: I sought, and there was none to give aid.

—*Isaiah 63:5* (c. 700 B.C.)

Chapter 1

SHORTLY BEFORE MIDNIGHT on August 2, 1981, a Panamanian-registered freighter called the *Primrose*, which was traveling in heavy seas from Bangladesh to Australia with a cargo of poultry feed, ran aground on a coral reef in the Bay of Bengal. As dawn broke the next morning, the captain was probably relieved to see dry land just a few hundred yards from the *Primrose*'s resting place: a low-lying island, several miles across, with a narrow beach of clean white sand giving way to dense jungle. When he consulted his charts, he would have realized that this was North Sentinel Island, a western outlier in the Andaman archipelago, which belongs to India and stretches in a ragged line between Burma and Sumatra. But the sea was too rough to lower the lifeboats, and so—since the ship seemed to be in no danger of sinking—the captain decided to keep his crew on board and wait for help to arrive.

A few days later, a young sailor on lookout duty in the *Primrose*'s watchtower spotted several people coming down from the forest toward the beach and peering out at the stranded vessel. They must be a rescue party sent by the shipping company, he thought. Then he took a closer look. They were small men, well-built, frizzy-haired, and dark-skinned. They were naked except for narrow belts that circled their waists. And they were holding spears, bows, and arrows, which they had begun waving in a manner that seemed not altogether friendly.

Not long after this, a wireless operator at the Regent Shipping Company's offices in Hong Kong received an urgent distress call from the *Primrose*'s captain, asking for an immediate airdrop of firearms so that he and his crew could defend themselves. "Wild men, estimate more than 50, carrying various homemade weapons are making two or three wooden boats," the message read. "Worrying they will board us at sunset. All crew members' lives not guaranteed."

If the *Primrose*'s predicament seemed a thing less of the twentieth century than of the eighteenth—an episode, perhaps, from Captain Cook's voyages in the Pacific—it is because the island where the ship lay grounded had somehow managed to slip through the net of history. Although its existence had been known for centuries, its inhabitants had experienced virtually no contact with the rest of humanity. Anthropologists referred to them as Sentinelese, but no one knew what they called themselves, nor what name they gave the island they inhabited—indeed, no one even knew what language they spoke. And in any case, no one within living memory had gotten close enough to ask.

The same monsoon-whipped waves that had driven the *Primrose* onto the reef kept the tribesmen's canoes at bay, and high winds blew their arrows off the mark. The crew kept up a twenty-four-hour guard with makeshift weapons—a flare gun, axes, some lengths of pipe—as news of the emergency slowly filtered to the outside world. (An Indian government spokesman denied reports in the Hong Kong press that the Sentinelese were "cannibals." A Hong Kong government spokesman suggested that perhaps the Primrose's radio officer had "gone bananas.") After nearly a week, the Indian Navy dispatched a tugboat and a helicopter to rescue the besieged sailors. The ship itself was bedded too firmly in the coral to be dislodged.

The natives of North Sentinel slipped off into the jungle as the helicopter approached. Watching from somewhere beneath the trees' canopy, they must have seen the whirring aircraft hover three times above the great steel hulk and touch down gingerly on the crowded deck. Thirty-one men—as well as one dog, the ship's mascot—were plucked safely back into modernity. Then the strange machines departed, the sea calmed, and the island remained, lush and impenetrable.

EPOCHS OF HISTORY rarely come to a sudden end, seldom announce their passing with anything so dramatic as the death of a king or the dismantling of a wall. More often, they withdraw slowly and imperceptibly (or at least unperceived), like the ebbing tide on a deserted beach.

That is how the Age of Discovery is ending. For more than five hundred years, the envoys of empire sailed through storms and hacked through jungles, startling in turn one tribe after another of distant human cousins. For an instant, before the inevitable breaking of faith, the two groups would face each other, staring. To be present at such an encounter seems, when we think of it now, to have been one of the most profound and astonishing experiences that our planet in its vanished immensity once offered.

But while such moments are about humankind's capacity for wonder, they are also, more often than not, about our species' capacity for inflicting immense pain. In those sudden flashes of baleful light, history has been written and histories erased, entire civilizations created and destroyed.

Each time the moment repeated itself at each fresh beach-head, there was one less island to be found, one less chance to start everything anew. It began to repeat itself less and less often, until there came a time, not very long ago, when there were only a few such places left, only a few sanctuaries still unviolated.

Now just one island remains. It is a place already all but known, encircled by the buzzing, thrumming web of a world still unknown to it, and by the mesh of a history that has forever been drawing closer.

MOST OF THE past ten thousand years of human history has slipped past North Sentinel, in the cargo holds of oared ships and the pressurized cabins of passenger jets. The island has almost wholly eluded all the devices and contrivances that have connected tribe to tribe, island to island, continent to continent. The written word. The compass and sextant. The steam engine. The radio. The smartphone. And no matter how much its inhabitants have managed to glean about the outside world from their glancing contacts—which is probably a good deal—there is no way they can know that their little home is the last place of its kind on this planet.

North Sentinel Island is not located in one of those parts of the world that are famous for having been "discovered"—the Caribbean, say, or the South Pacific. The Andaman Islands, though rarely visited by outsiders until the nineteenth century, have been known to Western civilization for much longer, albeit at the outer margins of cartographic consciousness.

In European maps, their shape long remained unfixed. Turn, one by one, those old hand-tinted pages: the small archipelago rises from the sea and scatters, changes colors and disap-

Columbus's arrival in the New World, October 1492. From Giuliano Dati, Lettera delle isole nuovamente trovate *(Letter on the Islands Newly Discovered), c. 1500.*

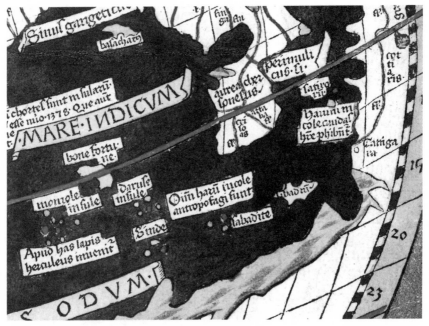

Detail of the eastern Indian Ocean from a map of the known world by Nicolaus Germanus of Ulm, c. 1482, based on the Cosmographia *of Claudius Ptolemy (c. 150 A.D.). An inscription warns,* Omnium harum incolae antropofagi sunt—"*The inhabitants of all these islands are cannibals.*"

pears, regroups and reemerges, like a school of fish in a tropical lagoon. Even as the contours of mainland Asia grow solid and precise—charted by mariners and geographers wending the fruitful shores of India and Siam—the Andamans' outlines never quite coalesce, for the islands offered very little to tempt the passing traveler. Even the archipelago's name is unstable—as if the outside world had discovered it, then lost it, then rediscovered it again, many times: *Caracuffaya. Dandemos. The Islands of Man. The Islands of the Satyrs. The Naked Land. Angamanain.* To this day, no scholar has resolved the question of how and when the islands came to be called Andaman, nor even determined the language and culture in which this strange toponym emerged. Still, those three measured syllables, deep and rhythmic as distant drums, suit the place somehow.

Then there is the oldest map-name of all, a name on late-medieval charts that derive, in turn, from those of the second-century Romano-Egyptian geographer Claudius Ptolemy. When I daydream about the islands, as I often do, this name comes into my thoughts more than all the others: *Insulae Bonae Fortunae.* The Latin phrase means *islands of good fortune*, and it also evokes a similar name from ancient times, the mythical *Insulae Fortunae*, or Isles of the Blessed, a paradise where Greek heroes, having passed three times through the Elysian Fields, dwelled in endless summer.

Even in long-ago days, however, the islands' reputation was mixed at best, and that auspicious name a queer anomaly. The very oldest Ptolemaic map also bears this blunt warning in medieval Latin: *The inhabitants of all these islands are cannibals.* For centuries, roving mariners would mutter hasty prayers, push their tillers hard, and steer well clear when they saw the green mounds of the Andamans float onto the horizon. None wanted to risk getting close enough that a monsoon storm might drive them ashore. Indeed, many believed it was better to founder in the ocean than try their luck upon those treacherous coasts.

Recorded history is only a small circle of lamplight in a dark forest of unchronicled human experiences—especially in a place like the Andaman Islands. What we call "discovery" and "first contact" are simply those encounters that were written down, mapped, photographed, or filmed. Surely there must have been many more moments of discovery and contact between the outside world and the Andamanese—including the Sentinelese—than those few that have left their mark on any surviving Western annals. Some of these may have been far more significant to the islanders, far more consequential in determining their attitudes toward strangers, than any of the episodes that imprinted themselves on the memory of the outside world.

Nevertheless, recorded history is all we have to go on. Here are some things that are documented as having happened in the course of the last thousand years or so:

In 1296 or thereabouts, Marco Polo described Andamanese generally as "a most brutish and savage race, having heads, eyes, and teeth like those of dogs. They are very cruel, and kill and eat every foreigner whom they can lay their hands upon." Historians believe that he based this on hearsay and did not visit the islands.

One night in 1771, an East India Company hydrographic survey vessel, the *Diligent*, passed by North Sentinel and sighted "a multitude of lights . . . upon the shore." During the island's brief transit across the western horizon, the British commander paused long enough to sketch its outline and bestow that name, the one it still bears on maps, reflecting how it seemed to stand sentinel at the upper end of a broad strait. This is its first recorded mention by any outsider. The surveying party did not stop to investigate, however. In those days, bonfires still beckoned from hundreds of coasts, all over the world.

In 1867, toward the end of the summer monsoon season, an Indian merchantman, the *Nineveh*, was wrecked on the reef off North Sentinel. Eighty-six passengers and twenty sailors got safely to the beach. On the morning of the third day, as these survivors sat down to a makeshift breakfast, they were suddenly attacked. "The savages were perfectly naked, with short hair and red painted noses, and were opening their mouth and making sounds like *pa on ough*; their arrows appeared to be tipped with iron," the *Nineveh*'s captain later reported. (The Sentinelese had probably scavenged the metal from flotsam on the beach, as they apparently still do today.) He had fled at the first shower of arrows and escaped with a few crewmen in the ship's boat, to be picked up several days later by a brig bound for Moulmein. The Andaman Islands were now officially part of the British Empire—the archipelago's largest island had been settled as a penal colony a decade earlier—so a Royal Navy rescue party was dispatched by steamer to the site of the wreck. It arrived to find that the *Nineveh*'s passengers had managed to fend off their attackers with sticks and stones, and the "savages" had not been seen since.

In 1896, a Hindu convict escaped on a makeshift raft from the penal settlement on Great Andaman Island. He drifted across twenty miles or so of open ocean and landed on the beach of North Sentinel. A search party found his body there some days later, rolling in the surf, pierced in several places by arrows and with its throat cut. No natives were sighted. After this, the island was left mostly alone for the better part of a century.

In the spring of 1974, North Sentinel was visited by a film crew that was shooting a documentary titled *Man in Search of Man*, along with a few anthropologists, some armed policemen, and a photographer for *National Geographic*. In the words of one of the scientists, their plan was to "win the natives' friendship by friendly gestures and plenty of gifts." As the team's motorized dinghy made its way through the reefs toward shore, some natives emerged from the woods. The anthropologists made friendly gestures. The Sentinelese responded with a hail of arrows. The dinghy proceeded to a landing spot out of arrow range, where the policemen, dressed in padded armor, disembarked and laid gifts on the sand: coconuts, a miniature plastic automobile, a tethered live pig, a child's doll, and some aluminum cookware. Then they returned to the dinghy and waited to observe the natives' reaction to the gifts. The natives' reaction was to fire more arrows, one of which hit the film director in the left thigh. The man who had shot the film director was observed laughing proudly and walking toward the shade of a tree, where he sat down. Other natives were observed spearing the pig, cutting off the doll's nose and ears, and burying both gifts in the sand. They did, however, take the cookware and the coconuts with evident delight.

In 1975, the exiled king of Belgium, on a tour of the Andamans, was escorted by local dignitaries for an overnight cruise to the waters off North Sentinel. Mindful of lessons learned the year before, they kept the royal party out of arrow range, approaching just close enough for a Sentinelese warrior to aim his bow menacingly at the king, who expressed his profound satisfaction with the adventure.

Nearly a century after the first unsuccessful attempts to photograph them, this may be the first time that any Sentinelese were captured on film. Still image from the documentary Man in Search of Man, *1974.*

A Sentinelese bowman aims his weapon at a helicopter, 2004.

In 2004, after the Indian Ocean tsunami, the Indian Coast Guard sent a helicopter to fly over the island and investigate whether the Sentinelese had suffered any casualties. Several natives were sighted, one of whom shot arrows at the helicopter. This was taken as welcome evidence that they had survived the disaster unharmed. The coast guard officers returned with a striking photograph: a figure runs across the beach, legs nimble as a dancer's, slanting his bow upward at the aerial trespassers. None of his features are visible, but the man's blurred silhouette, his tensile black body poised against the stark white sand, has the timeless immediacy of a Paleolithic cave painting. The image went out over international wire services and was published in dozens of newspapers. The world turned its attention, if only fleetingly, to a place it had so far overlooked.

But it wasn't until more than a decade later that North Sentinel at last won enduring fame—a notoriety that now seems destined to permanently ensnare it.

This is how it happened: In 2018, an American evangelical Christian—following, he believed, the summons of a god unknown to the Sentinelese—went clandestinely to the island. The would-be missionary, twenty-six-year-old John Allen Chau, had appointed himself to bring enlightenment to "Satan's last stronghold," as he called North Sentinel in his diary. He came equipped with a folding kayak to navigate the reefs, a waterproof Bible, various gifts (including a small soccer ball, safety pins, and freshly caught tuna and barracuda), and dental forceps "for arrow removal." Indian fishermen familiar with the nearby waters dropped him off a few hundred yards from shore.

Chau's evangelizing mission was not a success. On his first attempt at landing, he paddled toward the beach shouting, "I love you and Jesus loves you. Jesus Christ gave me authority to come to you. Here are some fish!" Sentinelese armed with bows and arrows chased him off before he could reach them. On his second attempt, he managed to get ashore, began singing hymns, and preached briefly from page one of the Book of Genesis. He tried to speak to the natives in Xhosa, a South African tribal language that he had studied at a Missouri school for missionaries, perhaps under the misapprehension that the dark-skinned islanders might somehow be related. Unimpressed, a young Sentinelese boy fired an arrow that hit the waterproof Bible. The point struck page 933, Chau later recorded. The verses were Isaiah 63:5 to Isaiah 65:2.

Once again Chau retreated, clutching the skewered Bible, losing most of his gear in the hasty getaway. Early on the morning of his third and final attempt, he scrawled a farewell message to his family before leaving the water-stained diary in the fishing boat:

You guys might think I'm crazy in all this, but I think it's worth it to declare Jesus to these people. Please do not be angry at them or at God if I get killed—rather please live your lives in obedience to whatever He has called you to and I'll see you again when you pass through the veil. Don't retrieve my body. This is not a pointless thing—the eternal lives of this tribe is at hand and I can't wait to see them around the throne of God worshipping in their own language.

Later, the waiting fishermen glimpsed a group of natives dragging a lifeless body across the sand. The young American had failed to advance more than a few yards into Sentinelese territory, let alone dislodge Satan.

Yet his brief visit bestowed another, distinctively twenty-first-century, kind of glory: within a few days, unbeknownst to the islanders, the fact of their existence went viral.

THERE SEEMS TO be no simple explanation for why North Sentinel Island was permitted to remain so isolated for so long. Certainly the natives' resistance to outside interference was well established many years before John Chau landed there with his waterproof Bible. In the long history of indigenous tribes' encounters with colonizers, however, mere inhospitality has rarely, if ever, proved a lasting obstacle.

It has been the good fortune of North Sentinel's inhabitants that their island is too small and inconveniently located to offer much enticement for colonization—lying, as it does, away from the main settlements on the east side of Great Andaman, the tight cluster of large islands, divided in a few places by narrow channels, that together form the main landmass of the archipelago. It has no natural harbors, and its surrounding abatis of uncharted coral reefs keeps out all but the most persistent or foolhardy seafarers. Those reefs also keep in the natives' unseaworthy dugout canoes, which they use only in the placid shallows of the lagoon.

North Sentinel long managed to elude even the nearly insatiable territorial appetites of the British Empire, which extended its fast-spreading Indian dominions across the Andaman archipelago in the 1850s and enjoyed unchallenged hegemony for nearly a century. An assortment of Englishmen—those incomparable observers and classifiers of the known world—took full advantage of the opportunities this offered to catalogue and describe their new imperial possession's countless exotic specimens of animal and vegetable life. Since the Andamans comprise nearly six hundred islands, large and small, with thousands of species that exist nowhere else in the world, the work begun then has continued to this day.

Initially, most of the larger islands were also home to various unfamiliar varieties of *Homo sapiens*, and as the British gradually made contact with some of the Andamanese tribes, they became the subjects of particularly keen interest. On the whole, the colonizers were not impressed by what they saw.

Unlike the mainland Indians, the black-skinned Andamanese were of a racial group that anthropologists of the time termed *Negrito*, a classification that comprised various indigenous communities scatted through remote areas of Southeast Asia. They lived as hunter-gatherers, subsisting mainly on fruits, tubers, fish, crabs, honey, wild pigs, and the eggs of turtles and seagulls. Some were so small, the Englishmen reported, as to appear almost Pygmies: adult males often measured several inches under five feet. The islanders wore no clothing and few ornaments; neither sex troubled to cover its genitals. (Indeed, Andamanese men often waggled their penises at interlopers, either humorously or as an apparent gesture of dismissive contempt, sometimes as a gentler prelude to drawing their bows.) Though they turned out not to be cannibals, they were easily mistaken as such, for they wore the jawbones—or sometimes even the entire skulls—of deceased relatives around their necks, a religious practice that many newly arrived visitors found unsettling. Most astonishingly, they had never learned to make fire, relying instead on the occasional lightning strike and then preserving embers carefully in hollowed-out trees.

In short, concluded the first official report to Her Majesty's government:

It is impossible to imagine any human beings to be lower in the scale of civilization than are the Andaman savages. . . . The little that is known of their manners and customs proves them to be without religion or government, and that they live in perpetual dread of the contact of any other race. Their origin is a mystery which will probably never be solved.

As unprepossessing—even repulsive—as the Andamanese natives may have seemed to the hardheaded colonial administrators, they provided first-class material for the burgeoning field of anthropology. During the first half century or so after the British arrived to establish their penal colony in 1857, a continuous stream of books, reports, and scholarly articles appeared, often accompanied by handsome photographic plates: silvery rotogravures in which naked tribespeople fished, danced, or brooded picturesquely over pagan talismans.

The few journalists and travel writers who occasionally ventured to the Andamans also found that the natives made satisfying copy for readers at home. Even by the usual low standards of nineteenth-century racism, the language in those articles was brutal. An English correspondent in the 1890s described the Andamanese as "men who, in their habits of living, are but few removes from the monkeys . . . with a quality of intellect scarcely expanded above idiocy, and a language of gutturals scarcely exceeding in range the grunt of hogs, the harsh scream of the jackal, or the whistling of birds."

But suddenly, unexpectedly, not long after the turn of the twentieth century, the scholarship and reportage slowed to a trickle, then largely stopped. The Andamanese, it perhaps seemed, were no longer considered a fruitful subject of investigation.

Another explanation also suggested itself: there were fewer and fewer of them left to investigate.

In 1857, it is believed, the indigenous population of the Andaman Islands numbered at least five thousand. In 1931, the last time the British tried to count, it was estimated at four hundred and sixty. As to the Sentinelese, the census-takers could only hazard a rough guess: perhaps fifty souls.

THE INHABITANTS OF North Sentinel Island are not the only remote, reclusive tribe to persevere into the twenty-first century. Experts believe there are still more than a hundred such groups, most of them huddled in the innermost valleys of the Amazon Basin, with smaller populations in the forested highlands of western Papua New Guinea. Statistically speaking, these citizens of terra incognita are a vanishingly tiny sliver of our species, at most ten thousand of the eight billion humans now on earth.

Yet none are quite like the Sentinelese, the only ones remaining who possess an island that is wholly their own. Survival International, the leading human-rights organization that defends the rights of indigenous peoples, does not hesitate to call North Sentinel's inhabitants "the most isolated people in the world."

Even the more approachable Andamanese tribes elsewhere in the archipelago remain enigmatic. The languages they speak have no apparent relationship to any other human tongue. No one knows how long they have been in the islands: people who live in huts made of palm leaves and hunt game with wood-tipped arrows leave few archaeological traces in a tropical climate. Their physical resemblance to certain African populations led some nineteenth-century scholars to conclude that they must descend from survivors of a slave ship shipwrecked in the archipelago. More than a century later, in the early 2000s, another generation of scientists hypothesized that the Andamanese might be living testimony to an early, previously unknown human migration out of Africa, one whose traces have been obliterated elsewhere by later waves of human settlement. Over the past decade or two, geneticists have managed to study DNA samples taken from an Andamanese tribe—the Onge of nearby Little Andaman Island—believed to be closely related to the Sentinelese, perhaps both culturally and genetically. The results are far from conclusive, but seem to demonstrate that the islands' natives share gene sequences with Aboriginal Australians, as well as with a few remnants of other tribes that survive in remote parts of Malaysia. What is clear is that their branch of the human species has been separate from others for as much as fifty thousand years.

Testimony from British times suggests that even then, the Sentinelese lived apart from other Andamanese, who considered them reclusive strangers: outliers among the outliers. No one can quite ascertain how, for centuries, they have apparently managed to maintain a static population size—currently estimated at perhaps two hundred people—on an island the size of Manhattan. Possibly they use some form of birth control; possibly they practice infanticide, as some other Andamanese tribes have been known to do. Surprisingly, inbreeding may be less of a problem than one might think: cousins marrying cousins have been the rule rather than the exception through most of human history. When I recently raised this question with one of the few genomic researchers to have studied Andamanese DNA, he told me that it's possible for a small group to maintain itself for a long time without any genes coming in from the outside. The Sentinelese, he speculated, might be a lot better off than the Hapsburgs.

There has been very little systematic scholarly examination of uncontacted tribes across the globe, nor of present-day first contacts. What we know is primarily based on scattered, anecdotal evidence, much of it gathered by activists, journalists, welfare organizations, and government policymakers. Still, certain common themes emerge from such reports. One is that few, if any, of these isolated tribes—or the scattered remnants of them—are fully isolated. Rather, they live at the margins of modernity, where neighboring tribes pass along both information and trade goods, like metal cookware or cloth. Moreover, they are actively monitored by the national authorities within whose borders they dwell. Police and natural-resource managers surveil them from helicopters and with satellite images, tracking their movements and population sizes, or venture into the borders of their territory searching for signs of human presence. The reasons for this are not wholly altruistic. In parts of the Amazon, areas where no indigenous people have been spotted within a certain number of years may be opened for clear-cutting—a problematic rule when dealing with migratory hunter-gatherers.

Another common theme is that today's "lost" tribes are usually not so much lost as they are in hiding: a matter of prudent foreign policy. Indeed, many of today's experts avoid the term "uncontacted"—which implies that those groups are still ripe for discovery—preferring "indigenous peoples in voluntary isolation." Surely this tactical withdrawal has to do with past encounters with the outside world that have gone unrecorded, or with warnings passed from other tribes by word of

ADAM GOODHEART · 25

mouth. In Brazil it was generally standard practice, as late as the 1970s, for frontier settlers to massacre any native people they encountered, flushing them out of their huts like quail to where other men crouched in wait with shotguns. Even groups that have avoided direct contact with colonizers can contract diseases passed from surrounding indigenous people who have not—or they can be subject to territorial pressure, and even violence, from others who are being pushed deeper and deeper into the forest. Their extinction can be imperceptible to the outside world.

For the past several decades, governments have more or less universally adopted national policies of noninterference with uncontacted peoples. These often exist more in theory than in practice, however, especially in places where untapped natural resources lie temptingly just beyond the margins of settled land. Changes in regimes can bring changes in policy. Protecting an indigenous group requires generation after generation of wise stewardship, and then suddenly the decisions of a single national leader—whether malevolent, corrupt, greedy, or just stupid—can change the course of a tribe's ten-thousand-year history. In Brazil, former president Jair Bolsonaro actively rolled back land protection orders that had previously shielded tribal areas from exploitation. "It's a shame that the Brazilian cavalry hasn't been as efficient as the Americans, who exterminated the Indians," he once said.

In the face of such seemingly inexorable forces, even outsiders who wish to protect remote tribal groups have begun to question the wisdom of absolute noncontact. Several years ago, a team of American academics published a scholarly article after scrutinizing Google Earth satellite images to identify forest clearings where uncontacted Amazon tribes might be living. They found that most were tiny—indicating very small populations—and only one had significantly grown over the course of a decade and a half.

"The reigning 'leave them alone' policy is misguided," these anthropologists argued. Instead, well-organized friendly encounters, in which native communities could receive food and supplies, vaccines, antivirals, and other medical care, would be more likely to ensure their continued survival. And "once a contact occurs, it becomes easier to protect native rights than it otherwise would be for an isolated population. Moreover, in our experiences from interviews with people after contact, there is a unanimous consensus that people stay isolated mostly because of fear of extermination and slavery."

Ultimately, the scholars said, the tribes deserved peaceful access to the outside world. Humans are a naturally gregarious species, intrinsically desiring the new ideas and opportunities that can come from meeting other groups. This curiosity and sociability—this profoundly engrained hunger for contact— might even be the only thing that could save them.

Vishvajit Pandya, an Indian anthropologist, has been study- ing the Andamanese for the past four decades. He is perhaps the only living outsider to have spent an extended period with islanders still following a traditional lifestyle, having stayed for fourteen months in the 1980s among the Onge people of Little Andaman. Pandya argues that when governments try to put security cordons around indigenous groups like the Sentine- lese, they are also hemming in the people they want to protect. "There's this romantic idea that they want nothing to change, and also that we can never understand them, even though we don't know the most basic things about life on their tiny island," he recently told me. "Nowhere in the world has there ever been a society that can survive in complete isolation, without any relationships of contact and exchange with groups outside itself. That's a bullshit notion of outsiders."

One can understand, of course, why the simple old myths still exert their appeal. The notion of a lost tribe both flatters and consoles the discoverers; it transforms them, in the telling, from gauche trespassers into honored guests. And some latitude has always been granted to the heroes of such tales: Did not even Columbus's discovery turn out to be fraught with qualifying footnotes? (He was neither the Old World's first visitor to the New, nor the first stranger to set foot on a Caribbean beach.) Were not Melville's noble Typees, by his own admission, already in hiding from the French colonizers of Polynesia?

Lost tribes, the anthropologist Stuart Kirsch has written, "are destroyed at the moment of their creation." That might explain why explorers have been so eager to create new ones, and why, now that the lost tribes of the earth are almost gone, we are moved to invent new ones beyond it. If there are none left in this world, there may still be, perhaps, dark places in the universe, where others live, like us and unlike, twins separated at a distant birth to show us what we might have been.

TYPE "North Sentinel Island" into a search engine today, and you can spend weeks reading articles, listening to podcasts, and skimming through blog entries, subreddits, and social media posts. You can zoom in close on images of the island taken from satellites, helicopters, and passing airliners. The Sentinelese have a seven-thousand-word Wikipedia entry, two different Facebook pages, several spoof social media accounts ("North Sentinel Island Department of Tourism," "North Sentinel

Island High School Marching Band"), and almost a quarter million Google results. They are featured in hundreds of You-Tube videos, with a cumulative total of more than a hundred million views.

The vast majority of these search results date from after November 21, 2018, which was the day that news of John Chau's death became public. The Indian fishermen had told a local friend of Chau about his apparent demise; the friend had contacted Chau's mother; the mother had contacted the U.S. State Department; and the State Department had contacted Indian law enforcement. The director general of police in the Andaman Islands then issued a press release headlined "Death of US National," detailing what was known of the situation.

Within less than twenty-four hours, the story was making news in outlets around the world and blowing up on social media. A few of Chau's fellow evangelicals mourned him as a martyr: a "fresh-faced missionary" who "burned with passion for the gospel of Christ." But most of the Twitter tweeters, Facebook posters, and Instagrammers saw his death as a well-earned comeuppance for religious bigotry, for tourist stupidity, for Western arrogance, for cultural imperialism, for habitat encroachment—or for all of the above. Even his father joined the reproachful chorus, telling journalists that his son had fallen prey to his own fanaticism and emotional immaturity. Eventually Chau received the dubious honor of a Darwin Award, which recognizes those who supposedly improve the human gene pool by removing themselves from it with a feat of spectacular folly or incompetence. Resting in his distant unmarked grave, the young man became far more vivid in death than he had ever been in life: a victim, a villain, a martyr, a joke.

As for the Sentinelese themselves, they became a meme

without—at least in the eyes of the world—ever leaving the Stone Age. By November 23, more than four thousand people had posted spoof Google and Facebook "reviews" of North Sentinel Island, many resurrecting the age-old depiction of the Andamanese as cannibals. ("The food wasn't that good. My right leg was supposed to be perfectly boiled but it was still a bit raw.") Many of their fellow humans hailed the islanders as heroes: staunch self-exiles from an interconnected world, the planet's most committed practitioners of digital detox. A few dozen naked tribesmen with handmade bows and arrows seemed somehow more powerful—more authentically human—than all those other billions of flabby bodies with iPhones in their hands.

Across the world, people of all political stripes found common cause with the islanders. Environmentalists and indigenous-rights activists swelled a chorus of outrage over any possible threat to North Sentinel's splendid isolation. On the other side of the spectrum, a right-wing member of the Australian Senate introduced a motion expressing solidarity with the tribe's "closed-border immigration policies" and unapologetic "lack of diversity." In uglier corners of the internet, white supremacists pointed to the Sentinelese as the world's starkest example of "negroids in savagery"—reprising a theme that stretched back more than a century.

THINGS WERE VERY different when I came across North Sentinel Island late one night more than twenty years ago, on the other side of the planet. It felt then—at least momentarily—like my own private place.

Along with many others at millennium's end, I was just

starting to discover a different terra incognita, with a still-unstable, optimistic name: the boundless virtual space that we called the World Wide Web. It is difficult now to reconstruct what it felt like to surf around online in those early days, as we began to learn new habits of mind—a listless form of exploration, a perpetual infinite browsing—that are now so deeply engrained. Harder, in some ways, than imagining the explorers of more remote centuries, setting sail for unknown worlds.

I was a few years out of college, writing for a magazine in Washington, and one night I stayed late at the office looking for something else—I no longer remember what—in an online database. I stumbled somehow across an article in a small scholarly journal, with an almost offhand reference describing a place I'd never heard of. This little-known speck of land called North Sentinel Island, the author reported, had recently been the scene of what was probably the last "first friendly encounter" in history. In 1991, an Indian government anthropologist, after more than twenty years of unsuccessful attempts, finally managed to interact face-to-face with the Sentinelese.

Intrigued, I searched online some more. That night in 1998, I found almost nothing: a few sketchy wire-service reports about the grounding of the *Primrose* and the home page of an evangelical organization in California that listed the inhabitants of North Sentinel (along with Buddhists, Jews, and "Gays in San Francisco") in its database of 1,573 "unreached peoples."

I remember how unreal the place seemed, that night in my fluorescent-lit cubicle, as I surfed on the oceans of information, the island emerging and then submerging again in the primeval digital sea, as on the ancient maps.

Then I looked up from the screen and out at the nighttime street. Black silhouettes of Washingtonians hurried past, toward the Capitol a few blocks away. A taxicab hissed over rainy asphalt. With a start, the thought hit me that life was going on *there*, too, at this very moment, on that distant island. Dawn would be breaking right around now over the eastern reaches of the Indian Ocean. A Sentinelese man, perhaps young like me, would be stirring from sleep and starting his day, just as I was ending mine. He was living not in irretrievable history, but at this moment, filling a human-size space nine thousand miles away.

I think that was when I knew that I would try to go there.

꙳꙳꙳ II ꙳꙳꙳

First Journey

1998

Boatmen off North Sentinel Island, 1998.

What is it to be admitted to a museum, to see a myriad of particular things, compared with being shown some star's surface, some hard matter in its home! . . . What is this Titan that has possession of me? Talk of mysteries! Think of our life in nature,—daily to be shown matter, to come in contact with it,—rocks, trees, wind on our cheeks! the solid earth! the actual world! the common sense! Contact! Contact! Who are we? where are we?

—HENRY DAVID THOREAU, *reflections on the summit of Mount Katahdin, Maine* (1857)

—

This was how a traveler reached the most isolated human settlement on earth, in the last years of the last century:

He boarded an evening flight at JFK for Heathrow, Air India 112, a plane full of elegant sari-clad women, London-bound businessmen, hippie backpackers. Then he caught another plane. He read the New York Times *while flying above the corrugated gullies of eastern Turkey, watched a Hindi musical somewhere over Iran. That night, and for the week that followed, he was in New Delhi, where the smog lay on the ground like mustard gas, and where one day he saw an elephant in the midst of downtown traffic.*

From New Delhi he went by train to Calcutta, where he waited for a ship—and for a ticket. There were endless lines at the shipping company office, and jostling, and passing back and forth of black-and-white photographs in triplicate and hundred-rupee notes and stacks of documents interleaved with Sapphire brand carbon paper. Next he was on the ship, a big Polish-built steamer crawling with cockroaches. The steamer passed all manner of scenery: slim and fragile riverboats like craft from a pharaoh's tomb; broad-beamed, lateen-rigged Homeric merchantmen. He watched the sun set into the Bay of Bengal, played cards with some Swedish backpackers, and took in the shipboard video programming, which seemed to consist of the complete works of

Macaulay Culkin, subtitled in Arabic. At last, on the morning of the sixth day, the ship sailed into a wide, sheltered bay—steaming jungles off the port bow, a taxi-crowded jetty to starboard—and arrived in the Andamans, at Port Blair.

In Port Blair, the traveler boarded a bus, finding a seat beneath a wall-mounted loudspeaker blaring a Hindi cover of "Macarena." The bus rumbled through the bustling market town, past barefoot men peddling betel nut, past a billboard for the local computer-training school ("I want to become the 21st century's computer professional"). On the western outskirts, at the airport, workmen were busy extending the runway—out into a field where water buffalo grazed—so that in a few years, big jetliners would be able to land there. A little farther on, the bus passed rice paddies, and patches of jungle, and the Water Sports Training Centre, and thatched huts, and family-planning posters, and satellite dishes craning skyward. And then, within an hour's time, it was at the ocean again, where on a very clear day you could see the island in the distance, a slight disturbance of the horizon.

Chapter 2

THE MAGNETIC TAPES are frail now, blurred by the passage of a quarter century. But when I listen today to the recordings I made of my hours of conversations with Dr. Triloknath (T. N.) Pandit, I can still make out the din of India in the background, a perimeter of sounds enclosing us: the bleating horns of auto-rickshaws and the cries of chai-wallahs from the alleyway behind my nondescript hotel; the comings and goings of tea trays and the soft automatic cough of the air conditioner switching on.

I had stopped in New Delhi to see Pandit on my way to the Andamans. The scholarly journal that first led me to the Sentinelese said that he was the government anthropologist who had made the first contact, seven years earlier. As I had done more research, I also discovered that he had published the only book ever written about North Sentinel Island: a slim volume from a small press in Calcutta, titled *The Sentinelese*.

It was not Pandit's idea to try to go there. He is not, by temperament, an explorer. (He had traveled outside India only once in his life, to attend an academic conference in Germany.) I did not understand this before I met him, and the stories I had heard of his experiences in the Andamans had led me to imagine a bearded, broad-chested man, swathed in khaki and bravado. Instead, Pandit was small and slope-shouldered, with a wispy mustache and gentle brown eyes. We sat in my hotel room and, over endless cups of milky tea—a conversation that ended up stretching over several days—he told me more about his life and adventures.

Pandit had grown up as distant from the Andamans as it was possible to go within his native country: in the Vale of Kashmir, amidst the western ranges of the Himalayas. The place he knew in childhood was a now-vanished India, a princely state ruled by a Hindu maharajah (a man descended, it was said, from the sun god). His family were devout Hindus themselves, Brahmans of high caste—"not kings, but the advisors and counselors of kings"—whose forebears had lived in the valley, at peace among their mostly Muslim neighbors, for many centuries. An English professor and noted Shakespeare scholar, his father also served as private tutor to the maharajah's son himself: a sleek black limousine would pull up in front of the house to take him to the palace. The Pandits' old brick house and formal garden bespoke their punctilious civility, stability, and proud sense of history. In the library, among his father's rare volumes in many languages, was a handwritten scroll that traced the family's bloodline through many generations.

That stability was deeply shaken in 1947, after the Partition, when the thirteen-year-old Pandit could hear machine guns in the distance as Indian and Pakistani forces battled for control of the valley. The maharajah abdicated and fled, replaced by a Muslim prime minister. But the old house, the garden, the library—the deep-layered bedrock of a family and its civilization—endured.

In 1966, when Pandit first embarked by steamer for the Andaman archipelago, his idea of what awaited him was based on the decades-old images of noble savages. Though he had paid no special attention to the Andamanese during his university studies—he had focused instead on the mountain tribes of his native Kashmir—Pandit had read one or two of the classic texts. And when, after applying successfully for a government job with the Anthropological Survey of India, he was posted to the islands, he thought he knew what to expect.

He found something quite different when he reached Port Blair, the Indian administrative capital on Great Andaman. The settlement had changed very little in the two decades since Indian independence, when the Union Jack that flew above the Chief Commissioner's residence was replaced by the new orange-white-and-green Indian tricolor. The penal colony had been disbanded, but the prisoners' descendants remained, an odd polyglot community of Hindus, Muslims, Christians, Sikhs. As for Great Andaman's original tribes, most survived just barely, in a state of squalor and neglect. A majority were mixed-race descendants of the original natives, communicating with one another in a patois of Andamanese and Hindi. In the main bazaar, a little dark-skinned old lady begged for alms outside a tea shop, singing ancient tribal songs in exchange for a few coins. Other Andamanese lived as squatters on the waterfront, in abandoned bunkers built during the wartime Japanese occupation.

Except for these survivors—some two dozen people in all—the ten tribes that British scholars had so sedulously documented on Great Andaman were now no more than a litany of names: Aka-Bea, Akar-Bale, A-Pucikwar, Aka-Kol, Aka-Kede, Oko-Juwoi, Aka-Jeru, Aka-Kora, Aka-Cari, Aka-Bo. Only one tribe in this part of the archipelago, the Jarawa, had managed to escape such a fate, by withdrawing into the remotest parts of the jungle and dealing ruthlessly with any trespassers.

No wonder Port Blair was considered a bleak post, a place where most government functionaries, including Pandit, arrived intending to stay and fulfill their assigned duties until reaching the next rung of the civil service. Against all expectations, however, he began to grow attached to the place. The plight of the Great Andamanese—which had become a collective term for all of the main island's tribes except the Jarawa—stirred his conscience. Even amidst their degradation, he caught glimpses of something ancient and noble. One day, an elderly man came to his office: Loka, one of the last full-blooded natives. They sat and talked—the old man spoke broken Hindi—and across the lines of caste and culture, an improbable friendship grew. Born sometime late in the previous century, Loka shared tales from his earliest youth, when studious Englishmen came among his people with their cameras and calipers. He spoke of his middle years, when Englishmen were fighting other light-skinned men and would come secretly at night, in their boat that traveled underwater, meeting him on the beach with cigarettes and whiskey to trade for information about the hostile tribe they called *Japanese.*

"It became a very personal relationship, not confined to my role as an anthropologist," Pandit remembered. "This was a man of great dignity and high integrity. Even in the shorts and old sun hat that he always wore, Loka's manner and body language commanded respect." Pandit dedicated himself to helping Loka and the other surviving Great Andamanese stitch back together the tattered remnants of their community. He arranged for the survivors to resettle a small island of their own, Strait Island, where the government provided food, clothing, shelter, and medical care as they relearned the habits of self-sufficiency and renewed their faith in themselves. Loka stepped into the role of a respected elder for the little tribe, teaching the younger members traditional dances that had long been forgotten. For Pandit, it was—as he later told me—an act of *prayaschitta*, the ancient Hindu sense of obligation to perform atonement and penance, even for the sins of those gone before. Even for the sins of the British, inherited by his fellow Indians along with the islands themselves; certainly for his fellow scientists, who had paved the way for the colonizers even as those colonizers paved the way for more scientists. He sensed that this mystical calling was somehow the reason that he had found himself in the Andamans.

Not long after Pandit's arrival, however, he began to hear vague reports of another, very different, native tribe, one he had not seen mentioned in any of the anthropological literature. By some accounts these people were small, dark, and smooth-skinned, like the rest of the Andamanese, while by others they were tall, fair, and bearded—descendants, perhaps, of escaped convicts from penal-settlement times. Everyone agreed that they were ferocious warriors. Strangest of all was that the island they inhabited, this unexplored place of myth and legend, was just a couple of dozen miles away, a few hours by boat from Great Andaman.

One day, after Pandit had been in the Andamans for less than a year, the governor of the islands summoned him for a meeting and announced that he was planning a large-scale expedition to North Sentinel, complete with armed police, naval personnel, and two large patrol boats equipped with inflatable rubber dinghies for navigating through the reefs. "There was a feeling that we were trying to establish friendly contact, which would be considered an achievement at the government level," Pandit recalled. He was offered the honor of being—so he was told—the first anthropologist ever to land on the island.

If friendly contact was its objective, the expedition failed. As the explorers approached North Sentinel, peering through their binoculars, they could make out several clusters of people, both adults and children, standing on the shore. But the moment they landed on the beach, the natives disappeared into the forest. Pandit and his companions followed as well as they could, with the police brandishing their rifles conspicuously. At last, after half a mile or so, they reached a clearing. There they found a group of huts, small lean-to shelters made of branches and leaves. Fires still smoldered outside each one. The huts were empty, and the unseen Sentinelese gave no sign of either welcome or resistance. Later, Pandit would speculate that they had realized that they were no match for the heavily armed invaders: "They must somehow have a clear idea of the power of the gun."

Pandit remembered that the contact party left gifts in the empty huts: plastic buckets, bolts of cloth, packaged candy. He remembered the festive air of the occasion—half military mission and half school picnic—and how, despite his protests, the policemen and naval officers took as souvenirs some of the household goods the Sentinelese had left behind: bows, arrows, a basket, the painted skull of a wild boar. His strongest memory was of the way the sunlight fell on the huts as he first emerged into the clearing from the shade of the jungle, filtering down onto roofs of leafy branches.

THERE ARE THREE small openings in the ring of coral that surrounds North Sentinel Island. Much of the year, even these are effectively closed, since during the monsoon season—which lasts from late spring through mid-autumn—the surf runs so high that any boat shallow-drafted enough to pass through would almost certainly be dashed to pieces.

From December to April, however, an unbroken spell of perfect weather settles over the Andamans. The air is warm, the skies are high and cloudless, and the sea, as travel books say, is gin-clear, reflecting immaculate beaches shaded by coconut palms. In the '90s, this was when the foreign backpackers converged on the islands—young Europeans, mostly, clutching their Lonely Planet guides, seeking a few weeks of sweet oblivion in beachside hostels well supplied with cheap hashish and expensive beer. This time of year is also the period when North Sentinel Island is exposed to incursions by sea. A large boat can anchor safely within a mile of shore, and then a small motor launch, guided by a skillful pilot who knows the territory, can—usually—make its way through the gaps in the reef to the beach.

During the 1970s and 1980s, T. N. Pandit made many such trips to the island. At first, the visits were sporadic, inspired by the whim of some local official or visiting dignitary who wanted to brave the arrows of the Sentinelese warriors. Pandit came along as an expert adviser on such missions, not as their instigator. He had his hands full on Great Andaman—figuring out how to handle the still-hostile Jarawa and also trying to aid the relics of the "friendly" tribes. Furthermore, he couldn't help wondering whether the Sentinelese, if successfully befriended, might not meet a similar fate.

The Indian government staked its definitive claim to North Sentinel in 1970, when a surveying party landed at an isolated spot and, atop a disused native hearth, erected a stone tablet proclaiming the island part of the Republic of India. Since the Sentinelese were not, and likely still are not, aware of the existence of either writing or India, it is unlikely that this monument has made much of an impression.

But not long after 1975—when *National Geographic* published, under the headline "The Last Andaman Islanders," dramatic photographs of the expedition on which the film director was wounded—trips to North Sentinel began occurring more frequently. No further visits by non-Indians were permitted. Occasionally, foreign scholars have applied for permission to visit the native tribes, but the Indian government is sensitive about the Andamans, and does not like outsiders nosing around. Jacques Cousteau once came to shoot a documentary on the islands and was chased away. Claude Lévi-Strauss asked Prime Minister Indira Gandhi to let his students do fieldwork among the Andamanese, and she refused.

Rather, North Sentinel became an attraction for curiosity-seeking Indian government functionaries, eager to have an experience that they could regale their friends with after returning to the mainland. If the Chief Commissioner of the Andamans made an exciting excursion to North Sentinel, before long the Deputy Commissioner would want to go as well, and so would the Inspector-General of Police. Since such bureaucrats were plentiful and rotated quickly through Port Blair, a steady supply of new dignitaries was always clamoring to go.

Anyhow, wasn't it merely romantic fantasy to think that the Sentinelese could maintain their isolation forever? The population of the Andaman Islands was doubling every decade, as the Indian government encouraged emigrants from the over-crowded subcontinent—Bengalis, Tamils, Sikhs, Punjabis—to settle there, joining the descendants of convicts brought by the British. As a "Tribal Reserve Area," North Sentinel was off-limits to outsiders, under pain of a prison sentence; Indian Navy helicopters and ships made regular patrols to keep anyone from approaching. The longer it stayed isolated, however, the more attractive it became to local fishermen, who occasionally visited its outlying reefs with a wink from the navy. Moreover, the Andaman archipelago was then, and sometimes still is, a haven for outlaws. Its thousands of miles of uninhabited coastline provided hideouts for gold smugglers, gunrunners, pirates, and drug dealers plying the clandestine trade routes of Southeast Asia. Illegal loggers came from Burma to cut valuable hardwoods; poachers came from Thailand to nab sharks, sea cucumbers, ambergris, and rare shells. The outlaws had fast boats and heavy weaponry, and they brooked no interference with their work. No one knew whether they had ever approached North Sentinel—or what unpleasant encounters they might have had with the island's inhabitants.

So there were ample reasons for the Andaman territory's officialdom to decide, as it did around 1980, that the Sentinelese must somehow be brought into its sheltering embrace. There was no need to repeat the mistakes of the past, not at this late date in history. The Indians were not the British; they had ample experience of the harm done by overzealous colonizers, and they believed that their hands were unstained by racial guilt. "Generations ago, we were all tribals," said one territorial governor. "Now nobody wants to go back. We got light, so let's spread it."

Beginning in 1981, expeditions were dispatched to North Sentinel every month or two during fair weather, laden with gifts intended to propitiate the fractious natives. Pandit and his fellow team members were given use of the Chief Commissioner's own official yacht, the MV *Tarmugli*. They would leave Port Blair after nightfall, double the southern tip of Great Andaman, and anchor off the reef at North Sentinel about six hours later.

The next morning, after breakfast, a contact party would set off toward shore in the *Tarmugli*'s motorized lifeboats.

On some visits the party would see Sentinelese; on others they would not. Invariably, however, they would try to land—at a place out of bowshot, if there were natives on the beach—and leave gifts. These included sacks of coconuts, bananas, and bits of iron conveniently sized to be hammered and scraped into arrowheads; often they brought special presents like mirrors, red ribbons, rubber balls, and bead necklaces. Sometimes the Sentinelese would make gestures that appeared friendly, waving their hands as the dinghies chugged across the lagoon; sometimes they would make gestures that were probably hostile, turning their backs toward the visitors en masse and sitting on their haunches as if to defecate. It was not out of character for them to rush out of the jungle and grab the gifts, then shower their retreating benefactors with arrows.

Occasionally there were incidents more reminiscent of *Police Academy 2* than of Captain Cook. Once, a high-ranking naval officer, newly deputed to the Andamans, accompanied the expedition. "He was a very fat guy, a Punjabi, with a very loud manner, and talking too much, that type of character," Pandit recalls. As the officer's dinghy approached shore, and Sentinelese were seen emerging from the forest, he stood up and started waving his arms over his head, shouting at the tribesmen in Punjabi: "Hello! Hello! I am your friend!" A second later, an arrow clanged against an iron shield that a crewman had held up, just in time, in front of the officer's belly. During another expedition, a boat carrying the superintendent of police turned turtle in the surf. Some armed Sentinelese watched from the beach, but did not shoot the struggling men. This was seen as an encouraging sign.

But still, by the early 1990s, after more than a decade of such attempts, the hoped-for breakthrough—the triumphant moment when the natives would "reach out and accept the hand of friendship," as local politicians liked to put it—had not occurred.

ELSEWHERE IN THE Andamans, Pandit and his colleagues had already gotten an intoxicating taste of what such an encounter might be like. Over the past couple of decades, they had used similar tactics to gradually establish friendly relations with the Jarawa, the one tribe on Great Andaman that the British and their Indian successors had not subdued. This was a matter of greater urgency than the Sentinelese missions. In the 1950s, the Indian government had established the Jarawa Tribal Reserve, a large expanse of virgin forest stretching from the fringes of the Port Blair settlements out to the big island's western coast. In theory, it would protect the tribe from interlopers. But now, as the Port Blair area's population rapidly grew, more and more outsiders were encroaching. The Jarawa fought back by shooting arrows at hunters, loggers, policemen, and road workers who entered their jungle—and, unlike the Sentinelese, the Jarawa rarely missed.

Even in the early days of British settlement, the Jarawa—reportedly darker-skinned and more ferocious-looking than most Andamanese—had gained a reputation as untamable. Long after the other tribes of Great Andaman had been more or less brought to heel, these elusive forest-dwellers continued to resist both peaceful overtures and more forceful efforts to gain mastery over them. In the 1870s, one resourceful colonial administrator proposed that the Jarawa should be taught to smoke, thus "establishing a craving" that only the British could satisfy. A well-armed expeditionary force was duly sent into Jarawa territory to deposit pipes, tobacco, and matches in the natives' huts. This failed to win over the natives. A few years later, the British managed to seize an elderly man and woman and bring them back to Port Blair in order to learn their language and "establish friendly relations." Disappointingly, these guests proved to be "surly and evil-tempered"—in fact, the man continually made gestures that suggested he was begging for his captors to strangle him or cut his throat. Only after the two began to grow sick with a persistent cough did the British at last reluctantly bring them back to the village where they had been captured.

Around the turn of the twentieth century—as outsiders intruded on their territory with increasing frequency—the Jarawa's defiance grew more aggressive. Sometimes they would ambush work gangs of Indian convicts sent out to cut timber. The British responded in kind with reprisals meant to deter the "marauders." They met with stiff resistance. On one such punitive expedition, in 1902, the young Englishman in command—Percy Vaux, Seventh Assistant Superintendent of the penal colony—managed to chase the startled inhabitants of a Jarawa village into the forest, capturing an infant and a small girl who had been left behind in the confusion. These he brought to one of the British settlements, for them to be cared for and educated in modern ways. Having completed this humanitarian mission, he returned to the jungle to finish chastising the natives. All did not go according to plan, however. A few days later, after happening upon another native encampment, the British drew fire from Jarawa bowmen. Vaux charged the assailants, machete in hand, only to be stopped short by a barbed shaft between his ribs. The Seventh Assistant Superintendent managed only to gasp, "For God's sake, take this arrow out of me," before expiring. The fate of the two children he had kidnapped is unknown.

Soon, the British went so far as to establish a special Indian constabulary, the Bush Police, whose sole duty was to patrol the Jarawa frontiers. But colonial officials still often joined the punitive expeditions themselves, often more for the thrill of the chase than for any reason of policy. The forest-dwellers, it was said among huntsmen in Port Blair, were the most satisfying game that the whole Empire had to offer—combining, in the words of one enthusiast, "all the skill and cunning of tigers and panthers and the intelligence of human beings." In the 1920s and 1930s, Englishmen sometimes returned from the jungle bearing the severed heads of Jarawa as trophies. (Indeed, despite the Andamanese natives' longstanding reputation for cannibalism and headhunting, Europeans are the only people in the whole history of the archipelago known to have resorted to these practices. On at least one occasion, shipwrecked mariners on one of the remoter islands, unable to survive by fishing or foraging, ended up eating one another.)

Even as the twentieth century passed its midpoint and punitive expeditions ceased under the gentler rule of independent India, the Jarawa who lived along the fringes of the outsiders' settlements seemed as stubbornly intractable as ever. They crept into neighboring villages by night and shot people, livestock, family pets, even the elephants used for shifting felled timber.

In the early 1970s, however, Indian officials launched a new effort to conciliate the Jarawa. Rather than focusing on those closest to the edge of the forest reserve, who seemed most sen sitive to encroachment, they concentrated on other bands of natives in the remoter coastal areas. The effort was led by both Pandit and Bakhtawar Singh, Deputy Superintendent of Police.

Singh—whom I would later meet in Port Blair—was a consummate civil servant. He had come to the islands as a teenage police recruit in the 1930s, loyally serving first the British, then the Japanese military occupiers, then the British again, and then the regime of postcolonial India. (He recounted for me, in ghastly detail, his memory of the public execution where his first boss, a British major, was beheaded with a sword by his second boss, an officer in the Imperial Japanese Army.) A hearty, strapping man with the beard and turban of a Punjabi Sikh, Singh was about as different physically from the Andamanese as it is possible for a fellow member of the human species to be. Yet the policeman felt drawn to the mysterious Jarawa and began leading expeditions by boat to the western beaches of the tribal reserve. He and his companions, often including Pandit, would undergo medical screening before their departure. Arriving at the coast of the northern tribal reserve, they would venture ashore to leave gifts on the sand—especially bolts of red cloth, which seemed to have a particular appeal to the natives. The Jarawa would retreat into the forest, but hurried down to the beach to retrieve the items as soon as the intruders had left. "It was like we were throwing corn kernels to birds," Singh recalled.

Eventually, the Jarawa seemed to start anticipating these monthly visits, which the Indian officials scheduled to coincide with the coming of each full moon. The contact party would arrive at the beach to find vines tied to the trees so that the offerings could be hung neatly above the sand. Years passed. Finally, one day in 1974, several Jarawa came swimming out and climbed aboard the approaching dinghy. Some scooped up the gifts, while others, smiling, embraced the delighted visitors. A new era seemed to have begun.

True, there were other Jarawa—those in the forests on the other side of the tribal reserve—who continued shooting villagers with undiminished zeal whenever an opportunity arose. But the coastal Jarawa suddenly gave up their warlike ways. When an official gift-bearing party arrived on their shore, it was like a joyous reunion. They even welcomed Pandit, Singh, and their companions to join them on the beach. Old video footage shows the jet-black natives swarming over the visitors' boats—men, women, and children, all naked, grabbing coconuts and bolts of red cloth, grasping the visitors' hands, reaching out curiously to pinch their light skin. Later, by the water's edge, they danced and sang, their voices joining in a strange, oscillating trill: *alay, oday, otalay, laday, alay, laylay, yamolay, alay* . . .

The anthropologists could not yet understand the Jarawa language. But there were other ways to communicate. "They loved to play with us, young and old, men and women," Pandit told me. "They thought nothing of climbing onto our shoulders, naked, to go for a piggyback ride down the beach. I remember once that I was running down the beach with two Jarawa girls, with a hand on each of them, on their shoulders, when one of them seized my hand and placed it over her breast as we ran. It did not seem sexual—just that it was perhaps a more convenient place for my hand to rest. You know, clothing and things like that are inconveniences of modern man." Indeed, before landing, members of the contact party would often strip down to shorts or underpants so as not to frighten the natives. Sometimes several Jarawa would surround a helpless scientist or policeman and, laughing, tear his clothes off.

There were a few deplorable incidents over the years. Once or twice, some young policemen and sailors tried to take advantage of the Jarawa women's innocence; the Indian authorities did not invite them back. Several young male Jarawa, in turn, once came aboard the *Tarmugli* and attempted to take certain sexual liberties with a female journalist from Bombay. The woman had to lock herself in her cabin until the frustrated men departed. And the natives would seize as a "gift" anything that struck their fancy, including jewelry, watches, and such. Pandit lost several pairs of spectacles this way.

Still, he remembered those visits as among the happiest days of his life: "As an anthropologist, such an experience is a matter of professional interest, but more than that, you are reacting as a human being, and as a member of the civilized world, so-called. It has been so exhilarating. One feels humble in so many ways in their presence. And I felt like I was traveling in time as well as space."

ON JANUARY 8, 1991, alongside articles titled "Poultry Training for Women" and "Oil Conservation Week Begins," the following front-page headline appeared in Port Blair's government-owned newspaper, *The Daily Telegrams*:

FIRST FRIENDLY CONTACT
WITH SENTINELESE

Four days earlier, a government contact party had paid a visit to North Sentinel, the first such expedition in more than a year. At first, as the anthropologists, constables, and officials approached the beach in the *Tarmugli*'s motorized dinghy, they could see no one on shore. Then, finally, a few Sentinelese stepped out from behind some bushes and started to gesture

Jarawa boy, South Andaman, c. late 1990s.

T. N. Pandit (left) with Sentinelese, 1991.

at the explorers, seemingly to indicate that they wanted gifts. As usual, the dinghy moved down the beach to a safe spot, and a crewman jumped out to drop off a bag of coconuts. The Sentinelese rushed down to grab it. But for the first time ever, they brought no weapons with them when they approached the water's edge—only mesh baskets and the iron-tipped wooden adzes they sometimes used to chop open the coconuts. Emboldened, the dinghy's passengers tore open another sack of coconuts and threw them into the water. Five of the Sentinelese swam out to collect the nuts, and a few others brought out one of their canoes. The contact team members gestured to them to come closer, but the natives got nervous and went back onshore. Deciding that they had taken enough risks for one morning, the explorers went back to the *Tarmugli* for lunch.

In the afternoon, however, some of them decided to return. This time, they found at least two dozen natives waiting for them. One, a young man, was holding a bow and arrow, which he pointed at the intruders, but a woman quickly came over and pushed the arrow down. The man took his weapons and buried them in the sand. At this, a great many of the Sentinelese started running down the beach and splashing through the surf toward the dinghy. The leader of the contact party, a small, officious bureaucrat with the title Director of Tribal Welfare, stood up and started personally throwing coconuts out to them. Then the Director leapt from the boat into the chest-high water—one of the young Sentinelese men recoiled in fright— and handed coconuts to the tribesmen as they crowded around. After he had gone through five bags of coconuts, he climbed into the dinghy, headed back to the *Tarmugli*, and returned to Port Blair to spread word of his triumph.

The news did not create much of a stir. There was some

back-slapping among the local officials and, later, a lot of internal squabbling over which one of them really deserved the credit. An editorial declared that the Director of Tribal Welfare was a very brave man, and the Indian government really ought to give him some sort of medal. The story went unnoticed by the overseas press, perhaps because foreign-desk editors were preoccupied that week with a story that seemed far more momentous: the impending war over Iraq's invasion of Kuwait.

T. N. Pandit missed the great event, too; he'd had a family emergency to take care of in Port Blair, so he'd sent two assistants in his place. A few weeks later, however, in February, he returned to North Sentinel with another expedition. This time, several Sentinelese men went so far as to climb into the dinghy and grab entire sacks of coconuts; one of them also spotted a policeman's rifle hidden in a corner of the boat and reached out curiously to touch it. Toward the end of the visit, Pandit was alone in the water with a group of Sentinelese; the other explorers had returned to the dinghy and started to drift away from him, and suddenly he found himself much nearer to the strangers than to his own comrades. One of the young tribesmen looked at him, scowled, pulled out an iron-bladed knife, and made a gesture, Pandit says, "like he was going to cut out my heart. Maybe he thought I was planning to stay on the island." But the dinghy quickly returned to pick Pandit up. He would return to North Sentinel several more times before retiring from the Anthropological Survey in 1992.

Pandit says he was thrilled, at first, by his encounters with the Sentinelese. "That they voluntarily came forward to meet us—it was unbelievable," he recalled, the last time we met at my hotel in New Delhi. "They must have come to a decision that the time had come. It could not have happened on the spur of the moment.

"But there was this feeling of sadness also—I did feel it. And there was the feeling that at a larger scale of human history, these people who were holding back, holding on, ultimately had to yield. It's like an era in history gone. The islands have gone. Until the other day, the Sentinelese were holding the flag, unknown to themselves. They were being heroes. But they have also given up.

"They would not have survived forever—that, I can reason out. On a scientific basis, we can say that this population might have lived for another hundred years, but eventually . . . Even destruction takes place in the natural course of things; no one can help it, it happens. But here we have been doing it in a very conscious way, knowing full well what the consequences could be. What would be and what could be are the same."

IT IS DIFFICULT—PERHAPS impossible—for us to know exactly how the moments of contact were perceived by the Sentinelese themselves.

Throughout the five centuries since the Age of Discovery began, Western travelers' fascination with first contacts has inspired them to chronicle, in great detail, their own experiences of such encounters. These accounts usually follow formulaic patterns, always self-flattering ones: Sometimes the brown-skinned savages, shouting war whoops, rain down volleys of arrows and spears upon the stout-hearted explorers. More often, natives are portrayed bowing down before the strange apparitions as if worshiping new gods, and marveling at the newcomers' vastly superior technology.

Yet some rare accounts from an indigenous perspective survive. Nearly all were transcribed by Europeans, interviewing members of a native group after they had established a means of mutual communication. Sometimes this happened several generations later. Still, the tendency of non-literate groups to preserve their histories carefully through oral tradition means that we can probably tease out some threads of authentic experience.

For instance, a missionary in the 1770s interviewed native elders whose primeval island had been "discovered" by Europeans in the previous century, when it lay at a remote edge of terra incognita. Tribal memory still preserved the details of that first contact.

One day many years ago, the elders told the missionary, some native fishermen were out in a canoe when they saw a dark, hulking shape drifting—or perhaps swimming—across the surface of the water. They hurried back to shore and alerted their countrymen, who gathered on the beach to watch the apparition drawing closer. Some thought it must be a sea creature; others, a very big canoe or house. Finally, the thing arrived and they saw that it was indeed a floating house full of white-skinned people dressed in strange colors, including a man clad all in red to whom the other strangers seemed to defer. The natives decided that this man must be "Mannitto"—which, the missionary parenthetically noted, meant "great or Supreme Being." Moreover, they decided that the other white men must be lesser gods accompanying the brightly clothed deity. They worshiped the Europeans accordingly, bringing offerings of food and other gifts.

That primeval island was Manhattan. (One thinks of Joseph Conrad's Marlow, watching the sun sink low above London: *And this also has been one of the dark places of the earth.*) The natives were a subgroup of the Algonquian Indians, who inhabited much of the region that is now the Northeast Seaboard of the United States. The year was 1609, and the man in red was Henry Hudson.

It appears that the missionary scribe in the 1770s misunderstood certain key details of what the Indians told him. In Algonquian cultures, the word *manitou* (which he recorded as "Mannitto") does not translate as "Supreme Being." Rather, it denotes, in the words of one historian, "the manifestation of spiritual power, a manifestation that could occur in almost any form." *Manitou* also means a numinous, all-pervasive force that can bring about sudden changes, for good or ill. The natives of Manhattan, then, were not worshiping Hudson and his companions, so much as greeting and welcoming them—probably with a degree of apprehension—as spirit-visitors.

In fact, scholars studying first contact experiences around the globe have observed that members of many indigenous cultures believe they inhabit a world teeming with supernatural beings that arise from the earth or sea, often in the shape of humans, animals, or the bleached corpses of the dead. Perhaps it is even misleading to call such apparitions "supernatural" in the way that Western cultures use the term, since the spirits are believed to be as real and as integral to the natural environment as any common rock or tree.

This human tendency to shape unfamiliar experiences into familiar narratives is probably universal. Think of the European explorers themselves, for whom each new land was another Eden; each fresh colony a rebuilt Jerusalem; each foreign culture a lost tribe of godless heathens, ready to receive the Book and the Cross.

One English anthropologist who worked among the Great

Andamanese a century ago reported that they believed in various special classes of spirits, known collectively as *lau*, who had originated from the souls of dead men and women. More specifically, the different groups included *lau* of the jungle, *lau* of the sky, *lau* of the sea. The *lau* of the sea, the natives told the Englishman, were grotesque creatures with pale skin, long arms, and bushy beards, who carried mysterious lights that could sometimes be glimpsed across the water in the darkness. Thus, the sudden appearance of light-skinned strangers with floating houses and fire sticks often does not challenge or overturn the natives' cosmology, but rather confirms it. The spirits are made visible; the shamans were right.

By now, a skeptic might note, it is unlikely that the Sentinelese—after so many contacts and near-contacts—would perceive intruders (whether John Chau, T. N. Pandit, or anyone else) as anything but fellow human beings, rather than apparitions from some realm of gods and magic. Certainly they have observed the outside world as intently as the outside world has observed them; more so, probably, since our boats and flying machines have by now become familiar parts of their surrounding world, and since hunter-gatherers are famously perceptive observers. They may not know exactly what helicopters or jet planes are, nor how they stay aloft—but, for that matter, how many of those jet planes' passengers could explain exactly how a million pounds of metal, plastic, and refined petroleum are able to lift them into the sky?

Still, this point of view is based on our own, rather arbitrary, distinctions between the natural and the unnatural, the human and the divine. Vishvajit Pandya, the present-day scholar who lived among the Onge tribe of Little Andaman, has noted that even after generations of frequent contact with British colonizers and Indian settlers, both they and the Jarawa refer to outsiders as *Ineny*, a term deriving from *ineny-lau*, the spirits who come from the sea. In the traditional Andamanese understanding, the spirit world is inseparable from the mortal world: humans and animals, natives and strangers, the living and the dead, all inhabit a shared space. What changes constantly are the power relationships among them. Just as humans hunt and gather animals, spirits—moving invisibly on the wind—hunt and gather humans. Human life is absorbed by the spirits; the death of one is the birth of the other.

AT EIGHTY-EIGHT, T. N. Pandit still lives in New Delhi, his body frail but his mind undimmed. I no longer need to make a pilgrimage to India to see him. We chat on FaceTime, he in his living room and I at my dining table with a mug of coffee, seven thousand miles away.

He has returned to the Andamans several times, most recently in 2014. Pandit is still remembered by the Great Andamanese, whose numbers have increased to seventy or so, several of them having taken spouses from outside the tribe. On his last visit, he was embraced by the grandchildren of Loka, the Great Andamanese chief, and by those grandchildren's grandchildren.

After John Chau's death, Pandit's phone rang constantly with calls from journalists all over the world, wanting to know about his own encounters with the mysterious islanders. "They seem to be my claim to fame, right or wrong," he says. As to the American's murder, the old man feels pity—and even, it seems, a tiny bit of respect—for this young man who, however foolhardy, possessed such stalwart religious faith that he was ready to sacrifice his life for it. More, though, he respects the islanders: "The Sentinelese gave the opportunity to him to go back alive. They were generous—they did not want him killed. I was there so many times, and even when they let us approach, they also told us not to come ashore. We obeyed but he did not."

Even before Chau's death drew the world's attention to the Sentinelese, Pandit's memories of them—and of the Jarawa—remained a living presence for him: "In my consciousness, they are always there." Occasionally they visit him in dreams. "Happy dreams. They have been part of my life for so many years. I gave no real gifts to them, but they gave a great gift to me." He vividly remembers the face of one young Jarawa woman as she sat in the explorers' boat, perfectly naked in the midday sun, carrying herself with the upright dignity of a queen. He remembers, too, the individual faces of men, women, and children who splashed toward him through the surf at North Sentinel Island—both their smiles and the sudden flashes of anger that convinced him to go no further.

Several years ago, a *New York Times* reporter interviewed Pandit and then published an article headlined "A Season of Regret for an Aging Tribal Expert in India"—implying that he had gradually come to repent those contacts with the remote Andaman tribes. This is not true, he says. Rather, his regret is about what he believes to be the islanders' inevitable fate. "My regret is that they will not remain forever. Their distinctive culture will cease to be. But are we also romanticizing a hard life that we do not know? The Jarawa invited us to come in; I say, let us wait for the Sentinelese to invite us. The day they want us to come ashore, we should go."

In the twilight of the anthropologist's life, his thoughts stray even more frequently to Kashmir, to the now-alien

world he was born into. The ruling princes are long gone, and
with them many of the landmarks of Pandit's youth. In 1990,
amidst the outbreak of fierce sectarian strife, his family members and most other Kashmiri Hindus fled for their lives. A
Muslim neighbor burned their ancestral house to the ground.
Pandit says he holds no rancor against the man, or against any
single perpetrator. His Hindu faith teaches that we inhabit a
universe propelled through a perpetual cycle of creation and
destruction, a wheel that turns for reasons only the gods know.
His scientific observations of human beings have shown him
that historical cataclysms often occur not through individual
decision-making, but with a kind of blundering violence that
lies almost beyond the reach of free will.

And yet the immutable truth remains that the home of his
forebears has disappeared from this earth. His father's library,
with its rare volumes in Hindi, Urdu, English, Sanskrit, and
Persian, has crumbled into ash. The ancient scroll with its
many generations of ancestors is irretrievably lost; those names
will never be read or spoken by Pandit's children, or by their
children's children. Thus a culture vanishes—an entire world
erased, with a single turn of the wheel.

Chapter 3

"You will find the Andamans very complex, very interesting," Pandit told me in October 1998, before I left New Delhi for Calcutta, where I would board the steamer to Port Blair. "In many ways, they are a throwback to the nineteenth century."

He was more or less right. My sense of traveling through time began on the ship itself, on the morning when, after five days and almost eight hundred miles, land appeared at last, far off our starboard bow, a faint, thin stripe at the horizon, just a few shades darker blue than sea and sky. This was the eastern coast of Great Andaman. About a hundred and fifty miles long and only a dozen or so miles wide, it is where the British situated their penal colony, and where nearly all the population of the Andamans lives today. Still, most of the modern development remains clustered around Port Blair, near the southern tip, and most of Great Andaman remains blanketed by trackless forests, as thick as they have been since time immemorial.

As the shore approached, I took out my telescope: an ancient, cumbersome thing, bound in brass and leather, that I had purchased on a whim in a cluttered curio shop in Calcutta—doubtless, I'd imagined, a relic of some long-dead Conradian sea captain. I unscrewed its lens cap and pointed it toward the thickening band of blue. The jungle now revealed itself, a fringe of treetops silhouetted against a higher, paler fringe behind, and then another behind that, higher and paler still. We edged slowly closer, past mile after mile of desolate beaches and rocky islets garlanded with surf. For many hours there was no sign of any human habitation. Then a few sudden flashes of sunlight on metal roofs among the trees, like signals from a heliograph, announced that we were reaching the outskirts of the settlements around Port Blair harbor.

Lazily, our big boat swung against the jetty, and at last we disembarked alongside a dingy passenger hall with a big sign reading "GATE WAY TO THE ANDAMAN & NICOBAR ISLANDS." The town beyond had winding, narrow streets thronged with mopeds, stray dogs, auto-rickshaws, pedestrians, bicycles, market peddlers, paan-wallahs, wandering cows, and just a few mud-stained cars. In the central bazaar, near a concrete tower with the town clock, was a Government Telegraph office. Outside one shop, I saw a poster that listed daily screenings at the archipelago's only cinema, a place quaintly called the Mountbatten Talkies. Most evenings, I would soon discover, the town's electrical grid suddenly failed, and for an hour or two, life went on by candlelight. But amidst Port Blair's rickety hodgepodge were also signs of a budding tourist industry. Half a dozen hotels had opened up, and in their lobbies stood racks of color brochures that advertised fishing trips, scuba dives, and nature walks.

It was still the season of the Indian Ocean monsoon, and even under the blazing midday sun, the air had a liquid quality, as if the world were a photographic print that had failed to fully emulsify. When the downpours came, as they did most afternoons, all this dissolved in an instant: a bombastic Hollywood special effect that should have quickly become routine, but still startled me every time.

I arrived half-expecting to learn the worst—that North Sentinel was already a stop on the ecotourism circuit, or that the local administration had stepped in and built a new settlement for the islanders, complete with a communal television set, as they had among the Onge of Little Andaman a decade earlier. Instead, there was much more surprising news: the island, for the first time in thirty years, was being left completely alone. The gift-dropping missions had ended in 1996. North Sentinel remained, like Prospero's island, a place where the air shimmered with invisible signals, with unseen Hindi soap operas and Thai music that drifted, unheard, across the Andaman Sea.

None of the local officials would give a clear explanation for why they had suspended the visits. I was chased out of offices, and bureaucrats whose job it was to set tribal policy told me it wasn't their job to set tribal policy. The most I could learn was that there had been occasional expeditions after Pandit's retirement, but that they hadn't always ended well. Several times, the Sentinelese had aimed their arrows at the contact party, and once they had nearly destroyed a wooden dinghy, hacking at it with their adzes. The explorers had never progressed much beyond the point of handing coconuts to the natives as they stood in the surf.

But when I went to the office of the Anthropological Survey and met Kanchan Mukherjee, the young scientist who now had Pandit's job, he told me something that, when I thought about it long afterward, seemed to answer some of my questions. "You're in luck," he said when I told him I had come to the Andamans to research the native tribes. "You have arrived here at a very interesting time. The forest Jarawa seem to have finally decided to end their isolation." The way he said this left me uncertain whether he was pleased about it or not.

I had already begun hearing vague rumors aboard the steamer from Calcutta, in conversations with Port Blair residents traveling homeward from the mainland. I hadn't been sure whether to believe them. Different passengers had told me different things about the islands' mysterious aborigines. One traveler warned me not to approach the natives because if they didn't kill me first with their poisoned arrows, they might bite me, and their bites were always fatal. Another man, when I mentioned my interest in North Sentinel, informed me that its fierce inhabitants were fair-skinned and bearded like Afghani Pathans—and six, seven, even eight feet tall. So when a third informant said that the fierce Jarawa had started coming out of the jungle and begging the settlers for food, I took it with a certain skepticism.

Now the anthropologist confirmed most of that story. The previously hostile Jarawa bands who lived in the thick jungles of the southern tribal reserve—the ones whom Pandit, Singh, and their team had never managed to befriend—had started making peaceful forays into modernity. But the Jarawa weren't starving, he said. Another motive, perhaps just as basic, was drawing them out: "They are exploring us, just as we are exploring them. These groups are, if you like, contact missions."

NOT LONG AFTER my arrival in the islands, on a Sunday, I went snorkeling at the Mahatma Gandhi Marine National Park, a cluster of islets off the west side of Great Andaman, a short bus trip from Port Blair. At the park's entrance, I boarded a ferryboat, along with a few dozen other tourists—mostly middle-class Indians from the mainland—and was taken out to a tiny, gloriously uninhabited island, where for the next few hours we had the run of the place. Honeymoon couples from

Calcutta held hands on the shore, while in the water the director of a mining company in Rajasthan paddled gravely back and forth, looking at tropical fish.

I'd heard that on clear days you could see North Sentinel from this spot, so I walked around to the part of the beach where I thought the view might be. The sky was too hazy, it turned out. But as I stood there looking, someone came up to me and asked, in broken English, if he could help. The man, who introduced himself as Bala, was Bengali, short, dark, and deep-chested, with a ragged fringe of beard. He lived, he told me, in one of the nearby fishing villages, and had worked as a shell diver until recently, when he began trying to earn a living as a tourist guide. I asked him if he had ever gone to North Sentinel.

"Yes, many times I am going," he said. "Never landing, staying offshore, two hundred meters, catching fish, catching shells. Sometimes seeing people."

"Could I ever go there with you?"

Bala laughed.

"No, too much danger. I go in fishing boat, coast guard helicopter coming, seeing me, waving, no problems. You come in boat, helicopter seeing you, coming, arresting. Very un-legal."

However, if I was interested in the Andamanese tribes, Bala told me, there was another place he could take me without running afoul of the law. He had some cousins who lived near a village called Tirur, up against the edge of the Jarawa Tribal Reserve. He'd heard from them that over the past few weeks, some Jarawa started coming out of the jungle and into the outskirts of the Indian settlements. If we went there, he could help me interview the villagers, and I might even see some natives.

So, several days later, we hired a Maruti minivan and a driver, ready to head up toward Jarawa country. I'd discussed my plans already with the anthropologist in Port Blair, and he'd suggested that on arriving in Tirur, I should check in with a certain Inspector Khan, who commanded the local unit of the Bush Police. This was the special force established by the British to contain the Jarawa—and half a century after the British left, it was still in place.

As I waited for Bala in my hotel's lobby, I noticed a sheaf of newspapers hanging from a string by a clothespin. A front-page editorial in that morning's issue of *Andaman Today* was head-lined "Administration should bring Jarawas to Civilised Life." It described some of the tribal people's recent forays out of the forest, suggesting that the island's government needed to step in and help these jungle people who were clearly eager to join the mainstream of modern India. News of the Jarawa's contact missions was spreading fast.

The road to Tirur started out well enough, on a straight course amidst the rice paddies and coconut plantations, through settlements named for obscure Englishmen who had inked these dots on some imperial map: *Collinpur, Herbertabad.* Less than an hour outside Port Blair, the road became a rutted track hemmed in by banyans and peepuls, palms and hibiscus. For some time it continued indecisively, not sure if it wanted to be paved or unpaved, before settling finally on un-. Past that point there were three more villages—no more than clusters of thatched huts by the roadside, really—and the last of these, the farthest outpost, was Tirur.

Our minivan pulled to a stop, and Bala leaned out the window to ask a villager where we could find Inspector Khan. The man said something in Bengali and pointed up the road. Bala translated for me: "He says tribal people is come and Khan *sahib* is go in van and sit by jungle."

After just a hundred yards or so, the road veered left into

a sudden narrow sunny valley, where it ended. Ahead was a single strip of paddy land, bounded by the great dark wall of the jungle, which was higher than I'd expected it to be, blocking half the sky. Right in front of us was an ancient, navy-blue police van, and next to the van stood two groups of men, apparently having a conversation. All of them were dressed in the faded khaki bush shirts that were ubiquitous in the Andaman backcountry. As we got out to meet them, one of the groups turned to go, and I noticed that these men were much smaller than the others. They were setting out single file down a muddy little path through the paddy toward the trees. Around their necks they wore odd fringes of brown fiber. The last one in line turned, waved, and smiled, teeth flashing preternaturally white in his dark face—and I realized at last that they were Jarawa.

They had come out of the jungle the previous night, eighteen in all, and camped by the edge of the rice fields. In the morning, the police had come to distribute coconuts and bananas, and some of the villagers, offended by the tribesmen's nudity, had given them old clothes to wear for as long as they were in the settlement. Now, the last half dozen Jarawa were making their way back toward the forest, carrying mesh baskets loaded with fruit. They waded across a knee-deep stream, and I saw that they were naked beneath the oversized shirts, their buttocks splashed with yellow mud. Every few steps they turned again, and waved, and shouted *"Milalay!"* and the people on the road shouted the same word back. This was one of the few words that the policemen thought they understood; it meant *friend*.

As the Jarawa reached the midpoint of the field, the rearmost of them turned and seemed to notice me for the first time—I was convinced of it—and smiled, and waved, and shouted, and before I knew it I was grinning like an idiot, waving and shouting too: "*Milalay! Milalay!*" Then their small dark shapes merged with the great dark mass of the jungle, and the valley was empty except for a few water buffalo and a sudden flight of white cranes, and I took my first good look at the *Ineny.*

KHAN *SAHIB*—A LARGE MAN with a paunch and a gray mustache—was the only policeman I saw in the group; the others were villagers. As soon as I had explained who I was and why I had come, they were eager to tell me about their recent experiences with the Jarawa. Although they had spent their lives mere yards away from the Tribal Reserve, few of them had even gotten a good look at a native until a few weeks before.

Tirur was settled in the 1950s by Bengali rice farmers displaced in the Partition, and ever since—like other frontier villages in the Andamans—it had come under occasional attack. The bowmen shot from hiding, often at night; if you got close enough to glimpse one, it usually meant that you were seconds away from death. In 1997, however, something unusual happened: three Burmese poachers came straggling out of the jungle, badly wounded, and turned themselves in at the local Bush Police outpost. They had been illegally cutting rare hardwoods deep inside the tribal reserve when the Jarawa ambushed them. Three of their companions were killed on the spot. The bodies were found by a police boat on the western beach of Great Andaman some days later; they lay in a row, horribly mutilated, facing the sea.

After this, the attacks on Tirur intensified. Half a dozen villagers (in a population of three hundred and fifty) were killed by Jarawa arrows, the latest one just this past March. She was an old woman, the mother of a local farmer, and she was working alone in his rice paddy, a field not a hundred yards from where we stood, when the Jarawa crept up on her from the forest. Her son found her, a little while later, with an arrow sticking out from—he gestured to show me—the middle of her chest. But after that, the killing had stopped. All was quiet until just a few weeks before, when a group of Jarawa had come out, unarmed and perfectly cheerful, and showed by signs that they wanted coconuts. Since then, more had come every few days, taking gifts before they went back into the jungle. No one knew why.

Clearly there were some differences of opinion among the villagers about their newly sociable neighbors. The man whose mother had been killed told me—to my surprise—that even though he could never consider the Jarawa friends, he was glad they seemed to have started becoming more civilized. Perhaps they could learn to live with the settlers in peace. Then his neighbor, a middle-aged farmer in a ragged lungi, interrupted. "Jarawa is like animals!" he said in broken English. "Jarawa only look at man, catch and kill him!"

When I'd finished talking with the villagers, we climbed into the minivan and followed Khan back to the Bush Police outpost. It was a simple structure with walls of bamboo lattice-work. On a table sat a kerosene lantern, a few empty cartridge boxes, a rifle that looked to be of World War I vintage, and a thick ledger book labeled "JARAWA MOVEMENT REGISTER." A radio buzzed with static in one corner. On another, higher, table, half-covered by a flower-printed cloth, was a small black-and-white television set. Most of his constables, Khan said, spent their days and nights in even more spartan surroundings, at a series of lookout posts deeper in the forest, spaced at two-kilometer intervals and raised on stilts among the trees.

He and his comrades were accustomed to living with dan-

ger. Khan crossed the room and opened the big brass pad-
lock on a wooden cabinet. Inside was a sheaf of three Jarawa
arrows. Two of the bamboo shafts were tipped with fire-
hardened wood; the third had a leaf-shaped head of hammered
iron. Khan explained that the natives used the expendable
wood-tipped ones when they shot from afar, to injure and dis-
able. Then they closed in and used a special iron-headed one
to kill. I took a closer look and tested it gingerly against my
thumb. It was ugly, but very sharp.

The government's contact missions to befriend the Jarawa,
Khan said—the joyful encounters that Pandit remembered—
had only a limited effect. Those expeditions had focused on
just one group, more than fifty miles north of here. Around
Tirur, the marauders had continued their raids on a regular
basis, often coming when the moon was full, usually in search
of metal for making arrowheads. The villagers knew to keep to
their houses during the brightest nights of the month. If the
Bush Police spotted Jarawa, they would fire blanks from their
rifles to chase them back into the forest.

A year or so earlier, those northern Jarawa started coming
into the settlements and asking for gifts. As they grew bolder,
they became more of a nuisance: stealing things from villagers,
sleeping in Bush Police stations, even, recently, boarding public
buses, much to the passengers' alarm. Not long before, several
had contracted chest infections that appeared to be viral pneumonia. The Andaman administration was at a loss over what to
do. As long as it had been the "civilized" people who were sending contact parties to the Jarawa, everything had been simple
enough. When the Jarawa themselves started sending contact
parties into civilization, matters had taken an awkward turn.

And now the long-feared southern Jarawa, too, the ones

near Tirur, had started to emerge from the jungle—perhaps after hearing about the changed circumstances in the north, the policemen surmised. An already complicated situation had become even trickier. The hostile standoff with these mysterious forest-dwellers had become almost routine after nearly a century and a half. Now nobody knew what would happen next.

Still, Khan said that he had no desire to return to the old days. One of his own constables had been badly wounded early that year in an attack on his forest outpost, perhaps by the same aborigines we'd seen that morning; the arrow's iron tip had entered his brain, poor fellow, and he was still in a rehabilitation hospital in Madras, with little prospect of ever leaving. Khan would rather give the Jarawa as many coconuts as they liked than have to face that again.

Then, too, he had experienced some interesting—even amusing—moments since the natives had become friendly. Just two weeks earlier, for instance, several had happened to come to this police station while the constables were watching television. At first, they'd stared at the set in amazement, but then after a few minutes they sat down—one of them cross-legged on the floor, two others atop Khan's desk—and started to watch. They laughed, pointed, talked excitedly in Jarawa. There was a Hindi film on the television, Khan remembered, and then a boxing match. They'd particularly liked the boxing match.

As I prepared to leave, the radio in the corner crackled suddenly to life, with a man's voice shouting urgently in Hindi. It was one of the bush outposts: the Jarawa whom we'd just seen leaving Tirur had stopped there and stolen some metal utensils that had been left outside. Let the tribals have them, Khan said calmly. Clearly he and his fellow officers were negotiating a delicate new balance of power with the forest-dwellers.

Later that day, after we'd left the Tirur police outpost, I asked Bala again, more urgently this time, about visiting North Sentinel Island. "Impossible," he said, shaking his head. "Too much risk." I pleaded my case yet again. And at last he looked up, shrugged, and said: "Is danger. Is risk. But I think we take risk."

BEFORE OUR TRIP to the island, I wanted to learn more about those northern Jarawa, fifty miles from Tirur near a village called Kadamtala, who had begun emerging from the forest two years earlier. If the coast guard intercepted me venturing to North Sentinel, I knew, I would be summarily expelled from the Andamans, and it would be wise to finish the rest of my reporting before that last, clandestine trip.

Back in Port Blair, Inspector Khan's boss, the superintendent of police, was surprisingly helpful, even offering to phone his colleague in Kadamtala, an officer named Ashok Kumar, on my behalf.

It took six hours by bus—a "Super Delux Motor Coach"—to lurch our way from Port Blair to Kadamtala on the Andaman Trunk Road, a single-lane highway that ran from Port Blair up into the Andamanese hinterlands. The road had been controversial when it was built, since a section of it ran through the Jarawa Tribal Reserve—but there was no other way for big logging trucks to reach the virgin forests in the northern parts of Great Andaman. At the last village before entering the reserve, the bus braked for a moment at a Bush Police barrier and an officer climbed aboard, taking a seat just behind the driver with a rifle propped upright between his knees.

We stopped a couple of times because of engine trouble, the driver and his teenage assistant disembarking with a wrench and the policeman with his rifle. After the second of these stops, we'd traveled no more than a few hundred yards when voices in the front of the bus started shouting, "Tribals! Tribals!" I heard the Jarawa before seeing them, a shrill trilling that blended with the excited cries of the Indian passengers. There were four of them, all naked—a man, a woman, and two children—leaping into the air like dancers, slapping the sides of the Super Delux Motor Coach and crooning . . . *woola-woola-woola-woola!* The driver barely slowed, but the teenage assistant leaned out the window and, grinning, high-fived the natives' outstretched palms as we passed.

At Kadamtala, I met Kumar at his high-ceilinged blue police bungalow, where we sat down for him to tell me about the emergence of the local Jarawa. Open on the desk in front of him was a school composition book with carefully written columns of Jarawa words and their Hindi equivalents, all gleaned from his recent interactions. The word *Jarawa* itself, he said, was based on a nineteenth-century Englishman's misapprehension; rather than being a collective name, it was a descriptor used by the Jarawa's neighbors, a now-vanished Great Andamanese tribe called the Aka-Bea, in whose language it meant *strangers*. The Jarawa called themselves *Aung*. This meant simply *the people*. They also drew distinctions between the forest-dwellers down near Tirur, whom they called *Boiab*, and the group in this area to the north, the same ones Pandit and Singh had made contact with, who were the *Tanmad*.

In Kumar's telling, the sudden transformation of the natives' attitude toward outsiders had happened thanks to one single, remarkable person: an adolescent Jarawa boy named Enmei.

Two years earlier, Kumar said, this boy had been out with a nighttime raiding party of older men when he fell behind the rest of the group, tripped over a tree root in the darkness, and broke his leg. Some villagers found Enmei two days later still huddled under the tree, shivering with pain, hunger, and fear. They alerted the Bush Police in Kadamtala, who brought him to the hospital in Port Blair. Enmei's injury turned out to be a serious compound fracture, and he was kept in the hospital for five months while his bones healed. "He was given the status of a VIP," Kumar said, his private room kept under twenty-four-hour guard. At first, the boy stubbornly slept on the floor and refused to put on any clothes, but eventually he took to using the bed and began wearing T-shirts and shorts. He even started watching television and wolfing down the candy that the nurses brought him. A quick learner, he picked up some Hindi and a few words of English.

There was great weeping and rejoicing among the Jarawa when the Bush Police returned him to his native settlement: Enmei's friends and family had all assumed that the *Ineny* had captured and killed him. Now he was a miraculous revenant, a local hero.

One evening a year or so later, some local Indian fishermen were working alongside the creek near Kadamtala when they noticed some unusual movements in a thicket of mangrove trees on the opposite bank. Approaching to investigate, they were surprised to find Enmei and half a dozen of his teenage friends, shaking the branches and waving to attract their attention. Soon a crowd of curious villagers had gathered. Someone brought bananas and coconuts for the Jarawa boys and girls, who were now grinning, delighted with their own bravado. As a crowning triumph, the police gave them a ride back up the creek in a motorboat, laden with gifts.

Since that day, there had never been another Jarawa arrow

loosed from the darkness; never another warning shot from the policemen's Enfields. Instead, groups of these northern Jarawa—men, women, children—came regularly down to the jetty for food and cheerful socializing. Thanks to Enmei, the members of his tribe now knew that if they had any kind of medical problems, they could come out of the forest and make their way to the Bush Police headquarters for effective treatment. Enmei's Hindi was improving, and several times he even brought a few of his teenage companions on the bus all the way to Port Blair to visit the doctors and nurses he had befriended at the hospital, serving as a tour guide and translator on these expeditions.

A couple of days earlier, in fact, the authorities in Port Blair had sent a health officer up to Kadamtala, and Kumar introduced us. The doctor, Ratan Chandra Kar, shared some observations that didn't completely sync with the rosy picture that Kumar offered. Dr. Kar had made his way to Enmei's home village and found that acute respiratory infections were now widespread among the Jarawa there, doubtless contracted from their recent interactions with the outside world. Some were suffering gastrointestinal problems from eating toothpaste or uncooked rice offered by well-meaning Kadamtala locals; others came down with skin infections from the secondhand clothes that the villagers gave them. Nor did all of their problems have to do with outside contact: Dr. Kar was also treating them for parasites, broken bones, and the bites of insects and snakes. The Jarawa's hunter-gatherer lifestyle, it turned out, was not actually so Edenic. And the medic confirmed the rumors that some of the indigenous people showed signs of malnutrition. The tribals' numbers had been increasing in recent years, while the deer and wild pigs on which they traditionally depended were

Jarawa arrows and basket at Bush Police headquarters,
Kadamtala, Middle Andaman, 1998.

"Two adult males demonstrating the shaking of hands when parting,"
photograph by Maurice Vidal Portman, Andaman Islands, c. 1893.

dwindling, most likely due to habitat encroachment by the settlers. Perhaps the Jarawa's recent overtures to the outside world didn't only have to do with the feel-good Enmei story.

Kumar was proud of the rapport that he and his colleagues had so successfully established with the formerly hostile natives. He showed me snapshots that they had taken with the Jarawa and artifacts that they had received as gifts—a basket, some arrows—and set them carefully on a chair for me to photograph. He was also delighted and somewhat astonished that I had sought him out after traveling so far. "My goodness," he said. "Washington to Delhi, Delhi to Calcutta, Calcutta to Port Blair, Port Blair to Kadamtala—and here we are!"

A constable whom I'd overheard talking on the radio in the next room now came in and said something to Kumar, who then turned to me, beaming. "Would you like to meet a Jarawa?"

"Yes, very much."

"Then you are very lucky. Mr. Enmei is coming."

A little while later, I found myself shaking hands with a boy of about sixteen—who, in his baseball cap, red T-shirt, and baggy shorts, might have walked down a street in New York or London without drawing a second glance. It took me a few minutes to notice that he also wore a bark-fiber fringe around his neck, under the T-shirt. He sat on a wicker loveseat facing my chair; a Bush Police constable brought him a mug of tea and some cookies. He was totally comfortable there, even the slightest bit disdainful as we looked each other over with appraising eyes. He seemed intent on showing me that he was in charge. Was I right to perceive a certain shrewdness in those eyes as well—the Jarawa teenager as Dickensian hero, alert to the main chance?

Kumar offered to translate if I wanted to ask Enmei some questions.

I realized suddenly that I had absolutely no idea what to say. Fumbling for a suitable pleasantry, I asked if he had traveled far to get here today.

No, not far, Enmei replied. The policemen gave him a ride in their jeep.

Is it true that the Jarawa come out to the settlements because they are hungry? Or is there some other reason?

No, there are pigs to eat in the jungle, and plenty of fish. But, he admitted, people do like coming here to get bananas.

Does he wear those clothes when he's at home in the forest?

Sometimes. He is the only Jarawa who does. He keeps two sets of these clothes in his hut, and a set that Kumar *sahib* lets him keep here. Enmei flashed a slight smile for the first time when he said the police officer's name.

Kumar helped Enmei to teach me a few words of his language, carefully checking them against the vocabulary list. *Umma*—father. *Kaya*—mother. *Ma*—mine. *Na*—yours. Enmei watched with only the faintest curiosity as I wrote these in my notebook. He looked with more interest at my wristwatch. (No, the policeman said sharply, he couldn't have it.)

Kumar told Enmei that I'd come there from a faraway place called America, and Enmei repeated it, *Mannika.*

At one point, Kumar was called into the next room, and I found myself alone with the Jarawa boy. He regarded me with half-closed eyes, as coolly blasé as any teenager. We had nothing at all to say to each other. I realized that he'd been getting very bored.

As soon as Kumar came back, Enmei stood up, ready to leave.

He turned to me and said the first words he'd spoken in English since we'd met: "Good night."

"Good night."

Outside, he climbed back into the constable's jeep, and the vehicle disappeared down the road in a cloud of dust. I'd just met my first Andamanese, a boy extraordinary for being so utterly ordinary.

ONE DAY IN Port Blair, I went to visit the Mohameds' scrap-yard. The Mohameds were five Muslim brothers from Madras, ship-breakers who were given a government permit to salvage metal from the wreck of the *Primrose*. They lived and worked near the waterfront in a big tin-roofed shed, a museum of the reclaimed junk of the twentieth century: huge rusty cogs and chains, oil drums and sections of hull plating.

Only two of the brothers were in when I went to see them, but they courteously offered me tea and shared their recollections of North Sentinel Island. They had visited the nearby waters sporadically for nearly a decade until 1997, often spending days at a time living aboard their boat, which they anchored near the freighter's hulk. On their first visit, some Sentinelese came down to the beach waving weapons, and even though one of the brothers waved a white sheet in response, the natives started shooting arrows, so one of the salvors' police escort fired shots in the air. Thereafter, the Mohameds worked unmo-lested. They often saw the tribesmen fishing from their canoes, and sometimes, on nights with a full moon, they would be awakened by voices singing around bonfires on the beach. The salvors never tried to go ashore.

"But one day," the elder brother related, "when I was work-ing on the *Primrose*, I saw something floating in the water, and I jumped in to get it. I can show it to you, if you want." He went upstairs and rummaged around for a few minutes in the loft that served as his bedroom, and when he returned he was carrying a Sentinelese bow. It was a lovely thing, tall and very slightly flexed, fashioned from the wood of some exotic tree. Its curved surfaces were broken into planes, long scraped striations from the adze that had shaped it. When I ran my fingertips along the concave side, they brushed against something rough: several tiny rows of zigzag lines incised into the wood. "You know," I blurted out, "if you ever wanted to sell this, I would give you, I don't know, six thousand rupees." It was the first sum that came into my head, but I knew it was more than most Indians earned in a month. The scrap dealer looked at me steadily. "No," he said. "Even my oldest brother has asked me many times to give him this. If I cannot give it to him, I cannot give it to you." Suddenly I didn't want the bow, felt wrong for having wanted it, but I smiled to show that I understood.

WE WENT TO the island a few days before I was to leave the Andamans. Bala told me he had arranged for a boat and crew; our cover story was to be that we were fishing, and if a navy patrol approached, I would duck under a tarpaulin and pretend to be a sleeping fisherman. To be on the safe side, we would leave under cover of darkness.

The afternoon before our departure, I packed up all the special outdoor gear I'd brought from America (synthetic-fiber camping shirt, sun hat, pen–sized flashlight, new camera), tucked the cumbersome telescope under one arm, and boarded a bus near my hotel and rode to a spot where Bala met me. We walked to his village, on the western coast of Great Andaman.

The little settlement of Bengali fishermen lay inside the

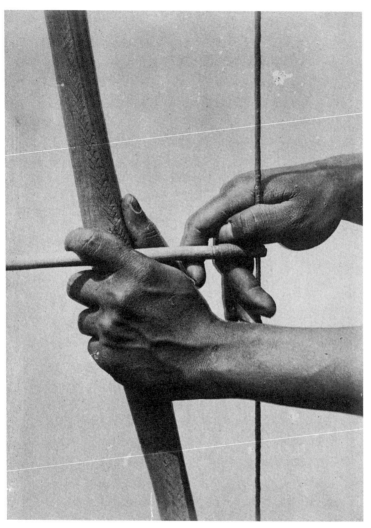

"Pair of hands demonstrating how to hold an arrow in a bow before shooting," photograph by Maurice Vidal Portman, Andaman Islands, c. 1893.

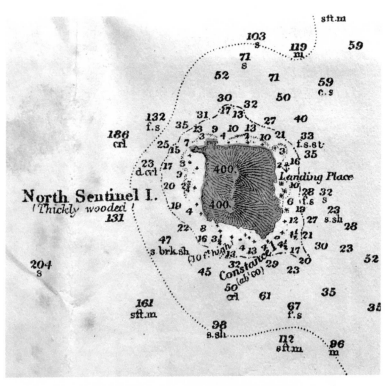

Map detail from Maurice Vidal Portman's A History of
Our Relations with the Andamanese, *1899.*

forest just beyond the edge of the sprawl around Port Blair. The footpath was unpaved; a big green monitor lizard sunned itself lazily in the middle and scuttled off at our approach. We dropped off my things and went down to the beach for a swim as the sun started sinking into the sea. Back at the village, I took off my shirt and shorts and washed off the salt with water from the communal cistern. I hadn't seen another living soul yet, but I was conscious of the many eyes that were likely watching me. My arrival there would be a big deal for his neighbors, Bala had said, but he'd asked them to give us privacy; he'd said I was coming so that he could take me on a moonlight fishing trip.

Bala's house was a cottage that he had built himself on land belonging to an uncle, a two-room structure with packed-earth floors and palm-leaf walls. He lived there with his wife and three sons, aged seven, four, and one. The house had no electricity and barely a stick of furniture, just bamboo floor mats that served alternately as chairs, tables, and beds. I horsed around outside with the boys a little bit before the eldest had to go in and start his schoolwork, which he did by the glow of an alcohol lamp as his brothers sat nearby, just watching as his pencil stub moved across the pages of a Hindi workbook.

The family gave me a real bed in the uncle's bigger house, vacated just to accommodate me. I tried my best to sleep amidst the noises of the village, familiar and unfamiliar: a cricket match on the radio, a mother humming to her infant, and the alien songs of insects. Just before drifting off, I caught a glimpse of two village girls peeping at me—the exotic stranger—through a gap in the bamboo partition.

An hour or so after midnight, Bala came in and shook me awake. I grabbed my knapsack and we walked in silence down to the shore, through groves of coconut trees thrumming with the noises of the tropical night. The moon was out, a pale half-circle ringed with cloud. The path through the trees was uneven in places, churned up by the passage of people and animals, so I reached for my flashlight, but before I could turn it on, Bala whispered sternly, "No torch. Moon is our torch." We continued until we reached a gravel road along the seawall, and there Bala left me, in a shadowed spot by the water's edge, and went down to the jetty to find the boatmen. I waited for a long time—looking at the stars, shivering a little in the night air—before he returned, so long that he startled me when I heard his footsteps again. He took my flashlight, pointed it out to sea, and switched it on and off quickly, twice. From somewhere in the distance, among the dark silhouettes of the inshore islands, came an answering flash, then the *chuk-chuk-chuk* of an engine.

One of the silhouettes seemed to detach itself and float nearer, and as it drew toward us the engine cut off and the dinghy glided up to shore. Bala and I waded through the water and climbed in. The fishing boat was small, less than twenty feet, and made of hand-hewn teak, with an inboard motor amidships. I could make out two figures hunched at the tiller, short and slightly built, like boys; they did not speak, but passed me a plastic tarp to keep close at hand. I took my place in the bow. There was no deck, no seat, just the hard timbers of the boat's frame. It was so narrow I could grasp both gunwales with my elbows bent at my sides.

The boatmen, who sometimes fished clandestinely off North Sentinel's reefs, had decided it would be too dangerous to go alone: if a storm blew up suddenly, or we had engine trouble, there would be no one to save us. So even though it meant splitting up the money I had offered to pay them—about three hundred dollars—they had brought a second boat. Off the far-thermost of the inshore islands we lay to; our flashlight signaled and was answered, and soon the other dinghy joined us, trailing somewhere astern.

Then for a long while there was nothing but the nearness of the warm black sea, the noise of the engine, and the white lines of our wake falling endlessly away. On this voyage there would be no raising or lowering of sails, no depth soundings, no sextant readings. The boatmen were steering by the stars, or by some private sense of direction; I couldn't tell. Bala wrapped himself in a tarp and slept. A light rain fell, and then stopped. Every so often, a spark leaped from the exhaust pipe of the inboard motor and tumbled into the sea, where it seemed to float for an instant before dying out. Once, I saw a faint reddish glint far to the west, like the beacon of a ship.

The clouds, high and scattered, were the first things to catch the rising light, then gradually the faces of the two boat-men, who I saw now were not boys at all, but men, skinny and bearded. One of them had a cloth wrapped, turbanlike, around his head. They spoke no English, and in any case the din of the engine made conversation impossible. I wondered what they knew about why we were going on this journey, and then I wondered what I knew about it, myself.

I crouched down and slept between the wooden walls of the bow. When I awoke a little while later, a red band hung over the horizon behind us—and the island, like its dark reflection, lay on the horizon ahead. Sheet lightning flashed beyond it, far away. I could now make out the boat that was following us; it was built in a traditional shape that I'd seen before in the Andamans, with a high, squared-off prow like a war canoe's. In both boats, the men had fishing lines out—it was our alibi, and besides, why not fish?—and every so often they would stop to pull in a tuna or a snapper, hand over hand, without tackle.

As we drew nearer to land, green leaves drifted past us, and the mangled limb of some tropical plant. From a stripe of neutral color, the island resolved gradually into a slab of beach piled high with trees—now visible, now invisible behind the swells. The closer it came, the more the sea around us sprang to life: dolphins leaped around our bow, flying fish skittered past, and startling turquoise shallows, crowded with corals, surged suddenly from the depths. The land itself still gave out no such signals; it was like a place where no one had ever lived, or ever would. The clouds above it looked more substantial than itself.

I took out my telescope—that absurd Edwardian encumbrance—and trained it as best I could on North Sentinel. We were as close now as we could safely come; a bulwark of breakers, ten feet high, rolled down onto the reef not far ahead of us, and two hundred yards or so beyond that lay the shore. Every tree trunk I looked at was a man, every piece of driftwood a beached canoe. But they were just trees and more trees, driftwood and more driftwood. Hoping to circumnavigate the island, we turned northward now and skirted the reef, and the incessant coastline unscrolled before us, like a loop of silent film.

Overhead, the clouds were thickening. When I'd planned my trip to the Andamans, I'd checked to find out when the monsoon season ended. Some of the guidebooks said October, others November. Because I was eager to make the trip, I'd decided to believe the ones that said October. They were wrong. It was now mid-November, and the monsoon season was still in full force. There was no phone or radio in our boat, of course, no life jackets. We were twenty-five miles from home, and had seen no other ships. And we were already taking on a bit of water through our hull. Every few minutes, one of the boatmen would stoop to bail with a plastic bucket.

Then Bala grabbed my arm. "Look," he said. "Tribal."

At first, I couldn't see the thing he was pointing at. And when I saw it, the dark shape looked too small to be a person, too small to be a tree stump, even. Then it stood up and walked across the beach.

Along this part of the shoreline, the forest grew high and dense, seeming almost to overhang the surf. The stranger—I couldn't tell from this distance if it was a man, woman, or child—had walked over to stand under the canopy, beneath a low, spreading tree. We cut our engine, and I stood up with my telescope. I glimpsed two other figures beneath the tree, their upper bodies in shadow, their bare legs shifting shapes against the sand. They were facing us, and one of them was holding something long and thin—a spear? A bow? Impossible to tell. I couldn't hold my telescope or camera in position with our boat riding the swell; the small circle of vision momentarily caught the group of figures, then swung wildly toward the ocean or the sky. The reefs allowed us no closer. We were too far to shout or signal, even if we'd known what to say. There was nothing to do but move on.

One of the boatmen started speaking now, explaining something in Bengali. Bala translated: "He say Burmese poachers come last year, take shells, shooting at tribal people. Before they came, tribal people—always waving. Now, always going back to jungle."

Our dinghy continued, with the other still trailing behind, across the north coast of the island, past dunes overgrown with scrubby bushes, and vapor rising from the jungle beyond. As we approached the far corner, I saw that it came to a point, with a tiny islet lying just offshore. The breakers here were higher than we'd seen elsewhere, stretching in an unbroken line along the reef, and just inside them another, smaller line of surf crashed against something else: a low barrier of blackened metal. It was the *Primrose*, pruned by the Mohamed brothers nearly to the waterline.

And between the *Primrose* and the beach, there was another boat: a Sentinelese canoe. It lay several hundred yards off, but we could see its profile clearly—a brown line above the water, with one figure seated toward the bow and another standing, poling, at the stern. They were probably fishing. I was sure they were watching us, though I now realize I could not possibly have seen that from such a distance. But beyond the impenetrable fence of surf, they were following a course like ours, westward alongshore, riding more easily than we were on their calmer patch of sea. For a minute or so the three of us were all parallel. I was standing in the bow—snapping pictures, scribbling notes—and saw our vessels click into alignment: two small fishing boats, with an upright figure in each, and between us, the dystopian ruin of the freighter.

This was as close as I was ever going to get.

Suddenly, I noticed that Bala was not paying attention to the canoe. He was staring in the other direction, seaward. "Look," he said to me, for the second time that morning.

It was a waterspout. I watched it in amazement: an elegant column, hundreds of feet high, drifting toward us across the gray pavement of the sea. Behind it, I saw, rose a wall of black clouds. "Is weather," Bala said. "Very, very bad danger. Now we go back."

The crewmen were shouting in Bengali, standing up and waving to the other dinghy: go back, go back. I realized what had happened. We'd just been rounding the northwest corner of North Sentinel, coming around onto the island's farther shore; there was nothing beyond it for hundreds of miles but the Indian Ocean. Now the weather that the land had blocked from view lay directly in our path. We reversed course and started to flee.

The dinghy made as much headway as its eight-horsepower engine could manage across the mounting swells. It was pitifully slow. After five minutes or so we all realized the effort was useless. The waterspout had disappeared now, absorbed somewhere into the shifting curtains of water behind it, but the storm front looked worse, and was coming up fast. The boatmen waved and shouted again, and this time they brought us around toward the storm. Bala explained: they'd seen a gap in the clouds—black wall on one side, black wall on the other, but a narrow gray defile in the middle—and our best hope was to try to run through it.

A minute or two later, the opening in the clouds slid shut. We could only ride out the lowering vengeance of the storm. The boatmen brought us up as close to North Sentinel's reef as they dared, pointed our bow at the advancing weather, and dropped anchor. They pulled out several blue tarps and ducked beneath, hunkering down in the bottom of the dinghy, and they gestured at me to duck under my tarp, as well. I preferred to see what was coming. I was more worried at this point about my notebook and camera than anything else, so I zipped them into my knapsack, wrapped it in the plastic sheet as well as I could, and cradled the unwieldy bundle in my lap.

The island was dark again, as it had been when we'd seen it in the distance at sunrise, but this time the sky was darkening too, and rushing to meet the land. The Sentinelese canoe had vanished. White streamers of mist that had lain atop the jungle reared upward, sucked by a sudden swift draft. For a moment everything was silent except the crashing of the surf, until the wind blew in. Waves struck against us; the line of breakers exploded like a train of powder. And then the rain came, aimed almost from the land itself; drenching the telescope, and the knapsack, and the Nikon camera, soaking through my clothes into my money belt and bleeding the ink of my passport; beating down on the island, and the wreck of the *Primrose*, and our nameless boat.

EVENTUALLY WE RAISED anchor, and the two boats turned homeward. For a short while, North Sentinel was still a looming presence at our backs; a few minutes later, I turned to take another look, but it was gone. For five hours longer, we fought our way through the storm before safely reaching Great Andaman, the weather finally abating. Bala and I staggered through the shallows and stretched out prone on the solid sand, side by side. My arms throbbed from gripping the gunwales and helping the boatmen to bail; my legs ached from bracing myself against the wooden hull; my mouth burned with the acid sourness of vomit.

Back at the little cottage, Bala's wife prepared a fragrant lobster curry that we could barely eat. When he and I were alone again, I unzipped my money belt and pulled out a thick wad of soggy rupees. Bala walked me to the bus stop, and a few minutes later I was back in what, over the past six weeks, I'd so often heard referred to as "civilization"—the paan stalls, and the travel agencies, and the gaudy shrines to many-armed gods, and the satellite dishes all craning their heads westward.

I was never able to get more information about the rumored Burmese poachers; the boatmen had evidently offered that story for Bala's benefit, not mine, and would share nothing further.

And that was it. I would go home with my journals, rolls of film, and telescope. I would turn it all into a long narrative that I could publish in a magazine, and a shorter version to tell friends and acquaintances for decades to come, a tale of wild adventure in an otherwise not wildly adventurous life. My experience in the Andamans became a story, then an anecdote, which in turn slipped, year by year, into a deeper past, the twilight of a receding century.

The island felt, finally, just as distant as it ever had.

III

Second Journey

1857 – 1900

"Adult male squatting on a mat,"
photograph by Maurice Vidal Portman,
Andaman Islands, c. 1890.

With regard to the photographing of savage races, the following hints may be of use.

The intending photographer has to ask himself the following questions:

Where is he going?

What is the nature of the climate there?

Will he be stationary, or a traveler, when in the country?

In what grade of civilisation and friendliness are the people he is going to study?

—MAURICE VIDAL PORTMAN,
"Photography for Anthropologists" (1896)

Where is there an end to the drifting wreckage,
The prayer of the bone on the beach?

—T. S. ELIOT, *"The Dry Salvages"* (1941)

Two young men in a photographic studio, at the edge of the jungle, near the end of the Victorian Age:

The first young man stoops under the velvet shroud of the focusing cloth. We can see only his legs. He has mastered his apparatus: the brass-bound mahogany box on its tripod, the red leather bellows, the fragile lens—Goerz's Double Anastigmatic, Series III—that he has preserved, miraculously intact, on a journey from the far side of the world.

The first young man works with the swift precision of someone who takes pride in his expertise. On his desk sits a nearly finished article that he will soon send back to London to be published in the Transactions of the Royal Anthropological Institute, *offering exact instructions for "the photographing of savage races." He recommends platinum prints, especially for his colleagues in humid corners of the Empire, like this one. More expensive than silver prints, certainly, but the platinotypes will be more permanent. Permanence is—given the unfortunate circumstances in this particular imperial outpost—of the utmost importance.*

The second man crouches a few feet away, naked, waiting.

The first young man looks at the second young man. He imagines the black skin metallic-white, fixed forever on a sheet of glass. He pulls a brass trigger on the side of his camera. The shutter drops like a blade.

In the dark box, the ghostly image blooms. A century and more hence—when both men lie in forgotten graves—this moment will still exist, captured in crystallized metal, like a single breath frozen on a windowpane.

Chapter 4

I'M A HISTORIAN now. My travels are more often in time, among the centuries, than between points that can be plotted on a map.

After my return from the Andamans in 1998, I never thought I would go back. But then, two decades later, the story of John Chau's death on the beach at North Sentinel revived my old fascination with the place. Incredible, I thought, that the islanders—perhaps the same people whose wavering figures I had glimpsed from the little fishing boat—were still holding out.

But before returning to see what had become of the archipelago in the twenty-first century, I decided to learn more about the islands' past. I wanted to know about all the history that North Sentinel had managed to elude, the fates that its inhabitants had somehow managed to escape. The island's uniqueness, after all, depended on what had *not* happened there.

My journey would take me deep into the nineteenth century, and to archives and libraries across three continents, among old papers and photo albums that sometimes still seemed to breathe the faintest exhalations of tropical damp and heat. What I found was a story of the British Empire—a saga not just local but also global, driven by rapidly shifting crosscurrents of science, colonialism, and racial hegemony. By the time I finished this historical journey, North Sentinel would no longer feel as romantic to me as it once did, nor as remote. Rather, I would learn, it was an island closely hemmed in by narrowly missed catastrophes, and by the best and worst instincts of our species: our greed, our lust, our thirst for knowledge, our will to conquer, our careless cruelty, our hunger for human connection.

ON DECEMBER 31, 1857—the last day of the last year before their world began to end—a group of Andamanese went down to catch fish off the beach at South Reef Island, a tiny islet in the northern part of the archipelago. They brought with them bows and arrows, nets woven of bark fiber, and seven outrigger canoes, delicate little craft that they had made by laboriously hollowing out the trunks of fallen trees. (Many of the possessions they were carrying that day are now in the British Museum.) Before the fishermen had a chance to push their boats out into the surf, however, they saw something strange in the distance: an immense black shape, half ship and half sea monster, coughing out great exhalations of dark smoke as it moved across the ocean. It was coming toward them.

The vessel was a small East India Company steamer, inauspiciously named the *Pluto*, that had left Calcutta several weeks earlier on a mission to investigate the Andaman Islands, particularly their suitability as the site of a new penal colony. On the Indian mainland, the Great Mutiny was in full blaze, and jails were overflowing with unfortunate captives who had raised arms against their British overlords. Despite the gravity of their assignment, the explorers had had a pleasant journey. Like many ships of its era, the *Pluto* was a kind of floating experiment in multiculturalism—its crew and officers included not just Britons but Irishmen, Italians, Maltese, Scandinavians,

Portuguese, Americans, Chinese, Africans, Bengalis, Burmese, Malaysians, a Frenchman, and an Arab—and in this case, the experiment turned out quite well. A Scottish sailor entertained his shipmates on the bagpipes; some Goan sailors formed an impromptu band; and the Arab boatswain strummed melancholy airs on his guitar. At Christmas, crewmen held sack races on the steamer's deck and boat races around its hull. The government officials on board—members of a special "Andaman Committee" appointed by the East India Company's directors—were also in a good mood, because they had already found a splendid site for a penal settlement (the future Port Blair) and were headed back to Calcutta with this happy news.

Their one disappointment was their failure, so far, to have any significant interaction with the Andamanese aborigines. There had been a few brief glimpses, a few arrows ineffectually fired, and that was all. So when the officials caught sight of the native fishermen on the beach at South Reef Island, they decided that here was an opportunity they did not want to miss. The *Pluto* hove to and lowered its longboats; the native canoes also put to sea and approached the steamer. As they drew closer, the chairman of the Andaman Committee stood up in the stern of his longboat and started waving a white pocket-handkerchief, hoping that the indigenes would recognize this international symbol of peaceful intentions.

A beautiful old lithograph freezes in time the moment before the two sides met. Sunlight slants down through high banks of cumulus clouds. The *Pluto* rides gracefully on the water, twin masts slightly raked, British ensign flying proudly at the stern rail. The longboats, bristling with oars, cut across scallop-edged waves. The canoes are little more than lines above the water, their passengers stick figures silhouetted by the sun. On the beach, more stick figures watch from beside a mound of jungle.

A moment later, everything exploded. The natives fired first; the Andaman Committee, an instant later. Three Andamanese were shot dead, including one warrior—a "chief," the committee later decided—who sank down in his canoe "almost with the dignity of Caesar." The survivors leapt into the sea and made for shore. All was chaos in the explorers' longboats as well: men howled in pain, some of them wounded by arrows and others by a volley of bullets that the second boat had accidentally discharged at the first.

And somehow, amid this confusion, an Andamanese ended up inside one of the European boats. It is not clear how he got there. The only contemporary sources are two conflicting accounts by the Andaman Committee chairman; one says that the man was seized as he tried to swim away; the other, that he grabbed a leather strap thrown to him from the longboat. Willingly or not, he fell into enemy hands, and was brought back to the *Pluto*.

Once aboard the steamer, at least, he does not seem to have struggled. The sailors promptly named the stranger "Jack Andaman," and dressed him in an old coat and trousers. (The clothes must have belonged to one of the cabin boys, since Jack, though a full-grown adult, was well under five feet.) One of the crewmen gave him a plug of chewing tobacco, which he swallowed; another tried to teach him, unsuccessfully, to smoke a clay pipe. Meanwhile, the members of the Andaman Committee earnestly debated what to do with him. They finally decided, in "the interests of humanity," to take him with them. So the *Pluto* got up steam and headed north again, with Jack gazing wistfully over the rail as the Andaman Islands slipped into the distance. The only thing that cheered him up was Neptune, the ship's dog, who came trotting over to sniff at him. Remarkably—for dogs were completely unknown to the Andamanese—Jack threw his arms around the animal's neck and began to caress it, and the two were inseparable companions for the rest of the voyage.

Back in Calcutta, eight hundred miles away, where the Andamanese warrior was kept in the Andaman Committee chairman's own house, he became an object of intense interest among his European hosts, and his spirits improved a bit. He was given a fine suit of clothes, shown off at tea parties, and taken out for drives in a carriage. A distinguished English physician introduced Jack to the viceroy, Lord Canning, as well as to Canning's wife, whom the curious stranger attempted to greet in traditional Andamanese fashion by blowing into her hand with a cooing murmur. (Her ladyship declined the honor.)

Afterward, Lady Canning wrote to her close friend Queen Victoria, describing Jack at some length. She remarked that he apparently possessed an uncanny aptitude for geographical orientation, even across great distances, never forgetting the exact direction in which his native archipelago lay. Lady Canning told the Queen about Jack's "delight and tenderness" at meeting an English child. But then the young native made a mysterious gesture. He looked at his English hosts, pointed his finger at the child, and then gestured in what he knew to be the direction of the Andamans. The physician informed Lady Canning that this must mean he had left a child at home.

Lady Canning concluded her letter: "It is very strange that those large islands, so near this place & Madras, should have languished so long in their savage state." If Her Majesty responded to this missive, her answer does not survive. One wonders what the habitually inquisitive Queen thought of that strange little faraway man, the newest subject of her Empire.

Jack was taken to visit a photographer so that his picture could be sent to the great German naturalist Alexander von Humboldt. Jack's keepers wanted him to pose naked for the camera, but by this time he had grown used to European modesty, so it took some effort before he acquiesced, and in the resulting photograph, he squints awkwardly into the lens. Still, it is recorded that when this picture was shown to its subject, he laughed heartily and exclaimed, "Jack!"

One night, however, after Jack had been in Calcutta for less than two weeks, he awoke with severe pains in his abdomen. A doctor rushed to his bedside and found that his case presented all the symptoms of cholera. Mustard poultices and blisters were applied, and after a few days the cholera seemed to pass, but by then Jack was also suffering from severe inflammation of the lungs. Earnest consultations were held at the highest levels of government (in the National Archives of India, there is a scribbled note in Lord Canning's own hand, inquiring anxiously about Jack's health), and it was quickly agreed that the unfortunate captive should return to his home. Since this meant depriving him of European medicine, it is odd that the British officials were so eager to relieve themselves of his presence—but in any case, they were. Nor, apparently, did anyone consider the possibility that he might transmit his ailment, whatever it was, to the other inhabitants of his native land.

So, by order of the viceroy, Jack was loaded with as many presents as he could carry—pots, pans, beads, mirrors, carpentry tools, cloth, thread—and put again aboard the *Pluto*. The steamer reached South Reef Island early one morning and, after a final set of anatomical measurements was taken, Jack was put ashore. (When the longboat approached, some natives were spotted watching from the beach, but they fled before it reached them.) By this time, his medical condition had worsened.

"It could not be ascertained," the *Pluto*'s surgeon reported, "whether he was pleased or not at being restored to his home." But the sailors made their affectionate farewells, unloaded the gifts, and set Jack's fine new clothes by his side, in a little heap on the sand. As they rowed back toward the steamer, they could see him standing there silently where they had left him, naked again on the beach.

ON A PLANET with almost no lost islands left—almost no human places unexplored—our true terrae incognitae can now be mapped in the geography of time. Nearly all of us, by the time we reach adulthood, have journeyed into a New World that would have seemed impossibly exotic to our childhood selves; reconstructing what it felt like even to live our own daily lives twenty or thirty years ago can be a challenge. (How exactly did I track down T. N. Pandit's phone number in 1998, or navigate the twisting streets of Delhi and Port Blair?) Novel experiences and devices scarcely have time to develop from miraculous to commonplace before becoming passé. Solid truths crumble; topographies dissolve and re-form. Each of us is Jack Andaman in Calcutta, again and again.

The future itself is now our looming, unseen shore, a blank map-space of marvel and menace, whose nature we try to discern from a drifting scrap of withered branch, or the stray echoes of drums in the middle distance. Forever present and unknowable; forever unreachable and inevitable.

When I started thinking about North Sentinel Island, I saw

it as a place somehow exempt from this conception of time, a place that both *was* history and also lay outside history. If not exactly a "Stone Age" place, as the newspaper articles and social media posts would have it, then at least a place whose inhabitants could dwell serenely in a moment that was both eternally past and eternally present.

This turned out to be a romantic notion—or at least a vast oversimplification. The Andamanese have a conception of time that is very different from ours, according to Vishvajit Pandya and others who have studied their cosmology. In their world, unlike ours, it is not something that humans progress through, moving from a vanished past into an unknown future. For them, time is not linear, but rather cyclical. There is no chronological math, no sequence of days and years that can be numbered. Events happen at the time of day when the wood dove sings, or at the season of the year when cicada grubs grow fat and sweet enough to eat.

The geography of history also has a radically different shape in the Andaman archipelago. Westerners use rivers and roads as metaphors for history. The native islanders, who know no such things as rivers or roads, use the wind. History travels to them, sweeping off the fathomless ocean, passing through them and among them, in breezes or cyclones, easterly or westerly, ceaseless and variable. The past abates, down to just the slightest stirring of breath, but will soon rouse itself.

This history is not chronicled in books, but rather written on the body itself: in painted designs of ochre and white clay, constantly erased and remade as the bearer's needs and circumstances change, as well as in ritual scarifications that remain indelible through an entire lifetime. Early photographers of the Andamanese sometimes noted that although most images

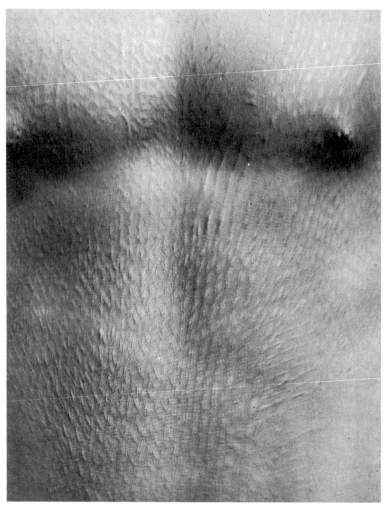

"Close view of a tattooed chest of a man of the South Andaman group of tribes," photograph by Maurice Vidal Portman, Andaman Islands, c. 1894.

The steamer Pluto arrives at South Reef Island, December 31, 1857.

"A girl wearing her sister's skull," Andaman Islands, c. 1908.

depicted them with smooth and unsullied surfaces, like Grecian statues, if you examined them close up, you would see intricate patterns of hundreds of healed cuts. In these scars were written the elegies and epics of the islands.

According to Pandya, the Onge of Little Andaman have no notion of a time when they lived in total isolation. The arrival of strange spirits on their shores—whether borne by good winds or ill—is as deeply engrained in their understanding of the cosmos as the wood dove's song.

The Onge, who began to have regular contact with British colonizers at the end of the nineteenth century, tell stories about that time, when *Ineny* came and there were many battles, when fire and smoke turned canoes full of men into stones. There was suddenly much more iron everywhere. People also started using unfamiliar leaves—tea and tobacco—and forgetting the leaves of their own forest, which made the forest spirits angry. There were more battles, more *Ineny*, more iron, and many, many more stones.

This disordered state is not permanent, a few tribal elders still say. The old balance of the world abides somewhere far away, and it will return, as history always does. The Onge must help make this happen by rubbing the iron against the stones. When the iron and the stones are both gone, then the deaths will dwindle and the births will increase; people will have no trouble finding wives or husbands; pigs will run in the forest and turtles will swim in the sea.

Pandya and other anthropologists have noticed that an Onge adult almost never sits still without scraping a piece of metal against a stone. They sharpen arrowheads and adzes over and over again, until the rock turns to powder and the iron's edge is thin as a leaf. But there are a lot of rocks in the world, and a lot of iron. Also, more and more *Ineny*. And not so many Onge.

So it is not true that the Andaman Islands—including North Sentinel—exist somehow outside of history, or that their history somehow began at the moment they were "discovered."

But, over the years, as I have read everything that I can about this experience of being "discovered," I have never quite shed the feeling that a century and a half ago, the Andamanese were snagged in history's wheel, plucked unwillingly out of one version of time and dragged fatally into another.

DURING MY STAY in Port Blair in 1998, I visited a small island that sits at the entrance to the harbor, and that, until the beginning of World War II, served as the local center of British administration. Ross Island was abandoned after the war, and the jungle had been allowed to reclaim it, with the merciless efficiency of tropical nature. Tall coconut palms sprouted from the mossy tennis courts, and vines had seized the pretty Gothic steeple of the Anglican church, pulling it roughly back toward earth. Already, the place seemed more like some ruined city of Olmec kings than like a settlement that thrived only decades ago. It was sweetly strange to think that in London veterans' hospitals or Yorkshire nursing homes, there probably lived people who in their youth hit volleys on those courts, or traded pleasantries with the vicar of that church.

But the best place to get a sense of the Andaman Islands under British rule is not in the archipelago at all, but rather in New Delhi, in the main reading room of the National Archives of India, among shelves crammed with indexes to the annals of the British Raj, their covers warped and stained by a century's worth of monsoon humidity. Opening one of these volumes to the section on the Andaman District and skimming the list of topic headings is enough to give the flavor of late-nineteenth-century life there:

> *Flogging to check unnatural crime in the Settlement of*
> *   Port Blair.*
> *Mortality among the sheep sent from Calcutta.*
> *Branding of life prisoners.*
> *Sentence of death passed on Bealalo alias Philip, an*
> *   Andamanese.*
> *Port Blair Superintendent applies for a large ice-machine.*

In the early days of the Andaman penal settlement, no important decision could be made without consulting the imperial authorities back in Calcutta. (The seat of power, along with most of its records, was shifted to New Delhi in 1911.) In the archives, therefore, still bound in their original dossiers of olive drab paper, are thousands upon thousands of pages of correspondence between the administrators in Port Blair and the masters of the Raj. No subject preoccupied these gentlemen as much, none generated as many pages of anxious inquiry and earnest recommendation, as the question of what should be done with the indigenous inhabitants of the Andaman archipelago.

British India was no longer what it had been a generation or two earlier, in an era of more worldly, cynical imperialists—freebooting merchant princes who went half native, and who were perfectly happy to let the locals continue burning widows and worshiping strange gods, so long as tea and spices flowed unabated to the East India Docks. As Queen Victoria's reign progressed, those sunburnt nabobs yielded gradually to a new breed of colonizers, an ever-revolving cast of bureaucrats from the mother country, determined to impose their own ideas of order and rectitude as they extended the bounds of British rule. Aboard the same India-bound liners came earnest gentlemen in clerical broadcloth, endowed with Oxbridge educations and propelled by earnest concerns for the corporeal and spiritual welfare of their heathen charges.

To such meddlesome men as these, the benighted state of the Andaman Islands seemed as much a blot upon the Empire as it did to Lady Canning. In 1855, on the eve of the Andaman expedition, one imperial functionary wrote of his astonishment that the archipelago "should be left in the possession of a handful of degenerate negroes, degraded in habits and intelligence to a level little above the beasts of the forest with which they dwell." Another huffed: "It appears highly discreditable in a civilised Government to allow such a state of things to exist."

Yet the penal colony's founders also knew that they could not afford to make enemies of the natives. They would have their hands full enough with another set of miscreants: the Indian prisoners sent out from the mainland.

So the British arrived in the Andamans bent upon dominion, but determined that their conduct would be above reproach. They did not behave like the Americans on the Upper Plains or the Belgians in the Congo, raping and butchering for sport. Nor had they any desire to repeat the unpleasant experience of their compatriots in Tasmania, whose ruthless expansionism led to the extinction of an entire race. As proper gentlemen of the Victorian Age, the archipelago's new masters were even determined to protect the chastity of local womanhood—and believed, initially, that Andamanese women would not prove sexually enticing to European men. (They based these hopes, in part, on what one of them delicately termed "an excessive development of fat around the gluteal region" of native females.)

Imperial policy was guided at first by the Andaman Committee's recommendations. In his official report, its chairman
had noted regretfully that the "wretched outcasts" occupying
the islands "are at present so savage or so ignorant as to regard
all newcomers as enemies . . . and to put themselves out of the
pale of humanity." In conclusion, he advised: "The contact
with civilisation in such circumstances, can only result in their
destruction, whereas, if they can be persuaded that no harm is
intended to them . . . [we can hope] that the means of reclaim-
ing and restoring them a place in the human family . . . may be
found."

The first British superintendent of the Andamans was therefore dispatched to the archipelago, in 1858, with unequivocal
instructions that the natives be treated with "the greatest forbearance and humanity," and that they be promptly informed
"that our intentions towards the people of the islands are of the
most friendly character."

That message somehow failed to get across. The problem,
at first, was that the Andamanese rarely let the Englishmen
come close enough to have any semblance of conversation. No
amount of gifts left in their huts would soften their hostility, let
alone bring them happily into "the human family."

A TRADITIONAL ANDAMANESE bow is an elegant, lethal
weapon—the most treasured possession of any native man.
Made from the tapered shaft of a young evergreen tree, it is
sometimes nearly twice as tall as the archer himself. The crafts-
man hardens the wood carefully over a fire, then shapes and
burnishes it with seashells until it is as smooth and finely curved
as a blade of grass. His arrows are long reeds of bamboo. For
millennia, these were tipped with shell or fish bone, but even-

tually the natives learned to craft arrowheads, spearheads, and adzes from bits of iron scavenged from wrecked ships. Beginning in 1858, that gave them an especially strong motivation to hunt down convicts from the British penal colony: they could kill a man, cut off his head, slip the ring and chain from around his neck, and thus immediately acquire a substantial prize of material for their weapons.

These instruments of death soon became all too familiar to both the British and their Indian prisoners. A native arrow, let fly at close range, could go straight through a man, and the shadowy Andaman jungles offered plenty of spots where bowmen could crouch, invisible to anyone just a few yards away. A surveying party would be out planning a road, or a team of convicts would be clearing jungle to make way for barracks, when the natives would suddenly attack them from ambush, murdering as many as they could before being driven off. To the newcomers, terror seemed to lurk at every moment, behind every rock and tree.

After every such onslaught, the British felt they had no choice but to organize a retaliatory raid. Soon the bamboo arrows, frightening as they were, proved no match for Enfield rifles. The casualty counts grew more and lopsided. In one engagement, seventy Andamanese were killed, and five soldiers received the Victoria Cross.

Often, some weeks later, fretful letters would arrive from the viceroy and his secretaries, urging renewed "conciliation and forbearance," reminding local authorities that "the Andaman Islanders, however low on the scale of civilisation, are British Subjects." But by that point the cycle had usually repeated itself.

Frustratingly, the indigenes were difficult to capture and

almost impossible to hold: "as slippery as eels," one superintendent wrote. One young native was seized after attacking a convict work gang, then trussed up for the night with a thick rope
to be taken back for punishment in the morning. Throughout
the night, the lad chewed silently and stealthily through the
stout cord, then made a successful dash past the sentry. An
entire brigade was turned out to hunt for him in vain. (They
"might as well have attempted to catch a fox," the superintendent explained to the authorities in Calcutta.) After that, the
British learned to use iron leg shackles.

Then, suddenly, the hostilities on Great Andaman ceased
almost entirely. There was one cataclysmic battle—fifteen hundred naked warriors came charging out of the jungle, straight
up against the guns of a British warship, with predictably
ghastly results—and after that, only a few desultory clashes.
Quite unaccountably, the natives started wandering out into
the settlement and behaving like friends: odd, bright-eyed little people whose merry air suggested that they had forgotten
there had ever been bloodshed. The Andamanese would ask for
gifts (coconuts, bananas, and, before long, tobacco and liquor)
and make amiable sport with members of the British garrison,
plucking at the soldiers' red coats and pulling on their whiskers.

But if the large-scale military clashes had ceased, they were
soon succeeded by a series of more intimate tragedies. One
awful incident in particular would irrevocably determine the
destiny of all those peculiar strangers.

KIDNAPPING INDIGENOUS PEOPLE is a practice that goes back
to the dawn of the Age of Discovery. On the day of his first
landing in the New World, Christopher Columbus wrote in his

journal of his intention to take six newly captured natives back to Spain with him "so that they can learn to speak." He also believed that his countrymen could convert them quite easily to Christianity, "for it seemed to me that they had no religion."

A few days later, two of the captives managed to escape and swim to shore, but the Spaniards later seized three women, five or six young men, and seven children. Later, a man who was the husband of one of the women and father of three of the children came onboard the *Santa Maria* and begged Columbus to let him join, a request that the admiral granted. Two months later, the little fleet set sail for Spain. Only eight of the captives survived the voyage, to be paraded through the streets of Seville during Holy Week. Soon, four of them were sick with European diseases. Nothing further is known of their fate.

ONE DAY IN early 1863, a small party of Royal Navy brigadesmen, who had been dispatched to an Andamanese camp "to establish friendly relations," returned to Port Blair with a shocking report. It seemed that the inhabitants had suddenly turned hostile, seized a sailor named Pratt, pinned the poor man to the ground, and shot him to death with their arrows as the other brigadesmen watched in horror. The soldiers loosed a volley or two of musket fire at the mass of agitated natives —several of whom dropped, wounded or dead—and made a hasty retreat to their longboat.

The colony's superintendent at the time was not a man to brook any such insubordination. Colonel R. C. Tytler was a hard-eyed, blunt-spoken martinet whose lifelong career in the Bengal Army—he had enlisted as a cadet at seventeen— accustomed him to far worse horrors than this. As a young

lieutenant, he had first seen combat in the Afghan War, helping avenge the notorious massacre near Kabul in 1842, when a
usurper king had slaughtered an entire British garrison after
promising safe passage back to friendly lines. More recently, he
and his young wife, Harriet—she eight months pregnant, with
two small children at her side—had narrowly escaped Delhi in
1857 when the sepoys mutinied. They had seen wagons laden
with corpses of slain officers; heard the screams of suspected
spies impaled on red-hot pokers; fled the city by night as their
house and all their possessions, together with the rest of the
army cantonment, went up in flames. The redoubtable Mrs.
Tytler gave birth in the back of a bullock-cart a few days later,
amid the din of nearby shellfire. (In appreciation of his wife's
sangfroid, the colonel later named the highest point in the hills
above Port Blair in her honor: Mount Harriet.) He had accepted
the Andaman appointment grudgingly, certain that something
better would come his way soon. Nothing did. His wife, despite
her fortitude in the retreat from Delhi, now languished in their
official residence, plagued by a relentless succession of tropical
ailments. Irritated and impatient, the Tytlers—like many British functionaries who ended up in that sickly and inhospitable
post—bore up as best they could, hating the place.

When news of Pratt's murder reached the colonel, he saw
it as simply another instance of native malfeasance, one that
demanded swift and severe justice. But Tytler was a man to
do things by the book, so instead of ordering a wholesale massacre, he wrote to the authorities in Calcutta suggesting that
the guilty Andamanese be captured and sent to the mainland
for proper trial. (In a letter, he referred to the Andamanese as
"a race of treacherous, cold-blooded murderers, assuming the
garb of friendship for the purpose of carrying out their dia-

bolical plans.") Within a few weeks, his troops had successfully captured the suspected ringleaders of Pratt's murder, two
native men named Tura and Lokala. With customary British
wit, they nicknamed the small, dark-skinned men "Jumbo" and
"Snowball," bringing them back to Port Blair in fetters.*

Then a fact emerged that should have changed everything:
Pratt had been in the act of raping an Andamanese woman—
Tura's wife, in fact—when he was killed. At this news, sharply
worded communiqués from the viceroy's council arrived on
Colonel Tytler's desk, ordering him to stand down from his
plans for "a general hunt against the aborigines," laden with
phrases like "unfortunate occurrences," "interests of humanity," and "much regret." But by that point, the two Andamanese were in the colonel's custody, and he did not intend to let
them go back to their own people. He saw an opportunity here,
and he intended to take it: only by civilizing these savages could
their race be properly brought to heel.

So instead of executing Tura and Lokala for their misbehav-
ior, the colonel simply kept them in fetters in the naval barracks
for several months—determined to punish any violent trans-
gression against a white man, whether provoked or not—then
released them from their chains and treated them almost as
honored guests. He had a special house built for them on Ross
Island, appointed convict servants to look after their needs, and
provided all the food and tobacco that they wished. He placed
them under the solicitous care of Port Blair's chaplain, one

---

* Here are some other names given to Andamanese in the nineteenth
century by the British, which I came across in various old documents:
Kiddy Boy, Ruth, Naomi, Joseph, Crusoe, Friday, Tarbaby, King John,
Moriarty, Toeless, Punch, Jingo, Sambo, Monkey, and Queen Victoria.
In this book, I have used actual indigenous names whenever those have
survived in the historical record. They usually have not.

Mr. Corbyn, a young Anglican priest with an Oxford divinity degree and impeccable references. This assiduous gentleman commenced teaching them basket weaving and the English alphabet, at both of which the two Andamanese displayed admirable aptitude. The only privilege that these natives were not allowed was that of returning to their homes and families.

Their keepers soon gave Tura and Lokala's special house a cozy-sounding name: the Andaman Home. Soon—perhaps unexpectedly—the two were joined by others. The British had always remarked upon the fondness that the Andamanese showed for one another, and their sorrow at parting from friends and relatives. Now it appeared that the men's loved ones must have been pining for them. One day, a woman and child made their way across the harbor to Ross Island. She was evidently Tura's wife—recently the victim of Seaman Pratt's assault—and the child was their son. The Englishmen dubbed the woman Topsy, after the enslaved girl in Mrs. Stowe's famous abolitionist novel. Before long, these new occupants were joined by others, until a dozen or more crowded into the Home. A pair of Andamanese were caught stealing crops from the colony's gardens: they, too, were sent to the growing establishment as compulsory inmates, followed by their families. So noticeable were the comings and goings of these unclothed visitors that the Home was soon moved to a less conspicuous location on Ross Island, lest the innocent eyes of Englishwomen be further polluted.

IN A REPORT to Calcutta, Colonel Tytler congratulated himself on the "firmness, decision, and kindness" with which the Andamanese guests were being treated. "They must see the superior comforts of civilisation compared to their miserable savage condition," he explained. "Though not immediately apparent, we are in reality laying the foundation-stone for people hitherto living in a perfectly barbarous state, replete with treachery, murder, and every other savageness." Then the colonel added: "Besides which it is very desirable, even in a political point of view, keeping these people in our custody as hostages." He assured his superiors that although the Andaman Home was now fenced in with stout bamboo palings and guarded by armed Indian soldiers, its residents "otherwise enjoy full liberty." Their orderly and submissive conduct, the colonel wrote, must surely "ripen into an intimate and warm attachment, and be productive of incalculable blessings both to us and to this benighted outcast race."

The Reverend Mr. Corbyn's progress reports were not so sanguine. Himself the product of a well-rounded English private education, he had resolved to treat his charges like schoolboys—which meant, in those days, that he would slap them smartly when they misbehaved. And as increasing numbers of natives were confined at the Home, they misbehaved more and more. Topsy would smear herself with body paint, then flop naked into an armchair, ruining the upholstery. One of the boys, rather than submitting cheerfully to instruction in his ABCs, seized a sewing needle and lunged as if to jab Mr. Corbyn's eyes out. Worst of all, these hellions showed none of the customary deference of Eton or Harrow boys: when he slapped them, they slapped back. Even when his pupils seemed better disposed, their behavior was often disconcerting, with the women sitting naked on the chaste young Englishman's lap—albeit without any apparent libidinous motives—and affectionately fastening chunks of coral to his necktie.

"Adult male drinking from a Nautilus shell," photograph by Maurice Vidal Portman, Andaman Islands, c. 1893.

"Adult male and female sitting on a mat, hugging each other,"
photograph by Maurice Vidal Portman, Andaman Islands, c. 1893.

"Andamanese group with Mr Homfray, their keeper, photographed at Calcutta," 1865.

*"Adult male sleeping on a mat; another man is squatting
behind him; they are wearing head and neck-ornament,"
Andaman Islands, c. 1893.*

"Mrs. Ford's Honeymoon group," c. 1895.
The two Andamanese men in front are identified as
"Moha" and "Daniel."

At last, the clergyman hit upon what seemed an excellent idea for subduing the Andaman Home's rambunctious inmates. He would impress upon them the manifold blessings—and the majestic power—of European civilization, in a way that he could not do in the rough frontier settlement at Port Blair: by taking a select group of them to the mainland.

Reaching Calcutta, Mr. Corbyn's eight travel companions—Tura, Topsy, a man nicknamed "Jacko," and five children—were received with even greater enthusiasm than "Jack Andaman" had been a few years earlier. To demonstrate British military might, they were taken on tours of the city's fortifications. To show off British technological prowess, they were shown the thundering steam-driven presses at the Calcutta Mint, then whisked aboard a railway car for a daylong excursion across fifty miles of countryside. To impress upon them the achievements of British scholarship, they were welcomed to a meeting of the venerable Asiatic Society, where they sat patiently while the learned members debated, at considerable length, whether it was advisable or even possible to civilize them.

They also became celebrities. Word spread quickly among the city's native and white inhabitants that cannibal "monkey-men" with long tails were staying in a house near the town hall. Within less than twenty-four hours, the building was thronged with Calcuttans clamoring to see them firsthand. Soon, the surrounding streets became impassable as curiosity seekers lined up all day for a glimpse of the picturesque visitors.

To the Andamanese, it must have been startling to realize that the world contained so many people, that they and all their fellow islanders were so vastly outnumbered within the immense galaxy of the human species. Frustratingly for Mr. Corbyn, however, they remained apparently un-awed by all the

military fortifications, steam-presses, railway cars, and scholarly gentlemen.

Exposure to throngs of gawking civilians had other consequences. Topsy was the first of the eight Andamanese to fall
sick. She eventually recovered a bit, but still, only half of the little group returned alive to Port Blair. Under circumstances only
vaguely described in the official records, two of them drowned,
one was "murdered," and one died "of natural causes."

Back at Ross Island, it became apparent that Mr. Corbyn's
project to subdue the intractable natives by exposing them to
the manifold blessings of civilization was having the opposite
of its desired effect. On his return, he acknowledged, he
had found their morale at its lowest ebb, and confided in his
journal—though not in his official report—that some of the
females appeared to have suffered "unwanted advances" from
the naval petty officer left in charge of them. Soon, the Home's
residents began escaping. Despite the stout fence, despite the
armed guards, they slipped away by night. Most managed to
swim the half mile to shore, some pushing their children on
makeshift bamboo rafts. They fled by ones and twos, then en
masse. One man even contrived somehow to get across while
still in iron fetters.

After a few weeks, almost the only ones left were Tura and
Topsy. She was still ailing, and he would not leave her behind.
Then, one night, he got into an altercation with the guards and
was hauled away in chains.

With her husband gone, the woman who had been called
Topsy at last made her escape from Ross Island. She crept out
of the Home under cover of darkness, slipped into the phos-
phorescent water, and started to swim. But her lingering illness
had left her too weak to reach the opposite shore. Her small

body was found on the beach a few days later, half covered by the shifting sand.

BENEATH THE HIGH-ARCHED Victorian ironwork of the Pitt Rivers anthropological museum at the University of Oxford, in a large glass vitrine labeled "Treatment of the Dead," amidst Egyptian sarcophagi fragments, Nicobarese funeral head-dresses, and an ancient Celtic mortuary urn, rests the skull of a person who lived and died in the Andaman Islands sometime in the mid-nineteenth century. Deep-socketed, daubed with dark-red ochre, and adorned with a delicate fringe of denta-lium shells, it seems even more deathly than ordinary human remains. Despite the jumble that surrounds it, this curio catches the attention of many museumgoers, and often appears a day or two later in the visitors' Instagram feeds.

Nothing is known about who the dead man or woman was, the family he or she came from, or the village where he or she lived. A shelf card from the 1880s records simply that the relic was donated to the university by one of the early overseers of the Andaman Home. It also explains that the skull was that of a "deceased relative" and that the mourner who wore it—prob-ably a parent, spouse, or child—did so to honor the departed loved one and also to ward off disease and misfortune, in keep-ing with native traditions. (Later anthropologists have come to understand this practice as deeply bound up with the native Andamanese concept of cyclical time and the enduring pres-ence of the past.) The card does not reveal how these cherished remains left the family's possession and came into European hands.

Early colonial officials, anthropologists, soldiers from the

local garrison, and occasional passing tourists all avidly collected Andamanese artifacts: by bartering for them, stealing
them from the natives' huts, picking them up from the ground
after skirmishes, or simply nagging and wheedling until the
owners were convinced to give them up. Those made with
human remains held a particular attraction, especially at a time
when scientists in Europe and America were beginning to make
serious study of the human body in all its ethnic variations. In
one of the Reverend Mr. Corbyn's reports, he wrote that despite
the natives' strong reluctance, he had eventually "persuaded"
them, "for scientific purposes," to let him take one especially
well-ornamented skull, probably that of "an important chief."

In fact, the skull could not have been that of an "important
chief," since the concept of a chief, or indeed a political ruler
of any kind, did not then exist among the Andamanese. Traditionally—indeed, among the Onge and Jarawa to this day—
decisions in the tribe are made consensually, with particular
deference paid to elders, both men and women. But this was,
of course, inconceivable to the loyal subjects of Queen Victoria.

Throughout the world today, one can find bits and pieces of
the nineteenth-century Andamanese, sometimes still on public display, but more often removed into deep museum stor-
age. There are four skulls at the Smithsonian in Washington.
A skull and mandible at the Museum der Kulturen in Basel.
Four skulls and five mandibles at the Royal College of Surgeons
in London. Another skull and jaw in Vienna. Three skulls in
Edinburgh. Two skulls at Harvard. Assorted human remains
in Chicago. In 2019, an Andamanese skull, evidently brought
home by a colonial tourist, was offered for sale on the website of
a high-end English antiques dealer.

No living Andamanese is known to exist today anywhere

outside the Andaman Islands. But those involuntary exiles can be found in a dozen or more countries.

ON ONE OCCASION in the late nineteenth century, according to an entry in the colony's official records, word reached British authorities that a Chinese junk, wending its way between Moulmein and the Strait of Malacca, had been shipwrecked on Little Andaman. The crew members were reported to have been captured or massacred by hostile islanders, so in due course a punitive expedition was sent out from Port Blair. The officer in charge was given specific instructions to capture some of the tribesmen, if possible, so that something might be learned of this previously uncontacted group's language and culture.

After a short battle that pitted native bows and arrows against British rifles—a fight which, the commander reported drily, "ended in favour of the Enfields and Sniders"—the invaders managed to seize one of the natives unharmed. Back on Great Andaman, the young prisoner was placed in the protection of a renowned Danish linguist who had come to the archipelago to study native tongues. The erstwhile warrior proved sufficiently tractable that he was given comfortable lodgings at the chief commissioner's villa, atop Mount Harriet.

Unfortunately—although "the greatest kindness was shown" to the prisoner—the linguist's investigation proved unsuccessful. One day, the Andamanese man happened to catch a glimpse of himself in a looking glass, and he responded with such alarm that his captors believed he thought he had seen a ghost, perhaps that of one of his own countrymen.

After that, the young man pined away. For a long time before his death, he spent entire days looking out from the summit of Mount Harriet toward North Sentinel Island, which was visible in the distance—as if it were his home, the Englishmen thought. Was it possible, they wondered, that he might somehow have come to Little Andaman from that other, even more mysterious, island?

He died before anything significant could be learned about his language, his culture, or even his origins.

NOTWITHSTANDING THE MASS escape of Andaman Home residents from Mr. Corbyn in the winter of 1864, the colony's superintendents continued to observe steady improvement in the relationship between the aborigines and their imperial masters. Eventually, the authorities built more Homes in the area around Port Blair—and remarkably, more and more of the natives began coming to live in them voluntarily. Many were enticed by tobacco and alcohol. Conditions in the forest were worsening, too. Andamanese villagers in the outlying areas never knew when they might return home from a few hours fishing in the lagoon to find that their huts had been stripped bare of utensils—all their painstakingly crafted bows, arrows, and ceremonial belts—by souvenir-hunting brigadesmen. Even the severe discipline and unappetizing fare in the Homes— meat from diseased cattle, "condemned" grain and biscuits— came to seem preferable.

But now the question arose: what to do with them? In some ways, their presence was even more nettlesome than it had been before. The Andamanese had certain noteworthy talents, but few that could profitably be applied to the needs of a colonial settlement. They were excellent bowmen, amazingly proficient swimmers (some could even shoot arrows accurately while treading water), uncanny mimics, and skilled jungle trackers, able to communicate across miles of forest by banging out signals on the buttress roots of certain trees. So the British put them to use hunting down escaped convicts—a reasonable occupation, though hardly enough to occupy them full-time. A few of the natives were employed as nannies, since it was quickly evident that they were remarkably affectionate with children, the Europeans' as much as their own. Others were kept as objects of amusement in Port Blair households, to be dressed up and coddled—at least until their masters' tours of duty ended, when they were left to fend for themselves. "The Government of [British] India," one official noted approvingly, "[has] adopted a policy towards the aborigines of the Andaman Islands which has made them, above all races of savages, the most carefully tended and petted."

An assortment of British experts—clergymen and educators handpicked for their intelligence and conscientiousness—were entrusted with the delicate work of "civilizing" them. They tried various techniques. Some, like Mr. Corbyn, did their best to teach the natives about clothing and the alphabet; others, attempting to win the islanders' trust, smeared themselves with ochre body paint and joined in the tribal dances. They didn't make much progress either way. How could decent social behavior be taught to people whose culture, the Englishmen believed, had no concept of individual property, privacy, or political authority? How could Christianity be understood by people who—while they believed in various spirits, both benign and malignant—evidently undertook no form of religious worship? How could math and science be imparted to people whose language apparently had no numerals higher than three? So the central Andaman Home eventually became a sort of souvenir factory, where residents passed the time sitting on the ground, making their traditional baskets, bows, and arrows for sale to English visitors.

At least the natives were not attacking settlers anymore. But the islanders' vitality had vanished along with their hostility. The first disquieting sign was what happened to their children: between 1864 and 1870, one hundred and fifty babies were born in the main Andaman Home, and not a single one of them lived past the age of two. Venereal diseases soon appeared and quickly spread. The history of the period can be summarized as a series of epidemics and dates, like a roster of military campaigns: pneumonia (1868), syphilis (1874), ophthalmia (1876), measles (1877), mumps (1886), Russian influenza (1890), gonorrhea (1892). When one of their number died, the Andamanese would weep piteously and embrace each other—the Home's superintendent found it "hideous, seeing grown-up men howling like children."

By the turn of the twentieth century, residents of the Homes were selling their ancestors' skulls as curios. In 1909, the English orchid collector and travel writer Violet Talbot Clifton visited one of the Andaman Homes. She immediately coveted a skull souvenir and was frustrated when the natives demanded the exorbitant price of three or four pounds each. After some persistence, however, she finally managed to obtain one of the ancestral relics "in exchange for a pair of khaki knickerbockers."

Throughout the first decades of British colonization, however, the inhabitants of North Sentinel Island remained out-of-the-way enough to escape the fates of their unfortunate cousins elsewhere in the Andamans. Indeed, no Englishman even set foot on its shore. Until, that is, the arrival of a very young, very strange *Inen*.

Chapter 5

Maurice Vidal Portman was, in almost every way, an unlikely imperial adventurer. In 2019, I contacted his closest surviving relative, a retired British Army colonel living in rural Devonshire. "What I don't understand is how on earth my great-uncle ever ended up in a place like the Andaman Islands," the genial ex-officer told me. "I mean, all the rest of the Portmans just didn't do very much. Except for him, my ancestors were extraordinarily dull."

They were also extraordinarily rich. So rich, in fact, that the Andaman explorer's grandfather, the resplendently named Lord Edward Berkeley Portman, First Viscount Portman of Bryanston, was among the wealthiest aristocrats in Britain, and some of his descendants have remained so to this day. Their fortune goes back to the reign of Henry VIII, when a providential forebear acquired a small farm, a hundred acres or so of orchards and meadows just outside London's medieval walls. By the nineteenth century, that farmland—still in the family— had become a hundred acres or so of Marylebone, a posh residential district in the heart of the West End. When I recently visited the sleek, modern headquarters of the Portman Estate, overlooking the gated oasis of Portman Square, an employee of the current viscount brought out several richly bound family scrapbooks from the 1880s and 1890s. There was nothing in them about the Andaman Islands, but hundreds of newspaper cuttings chronicled an incessant round of balls, banquets, fox hunts, society christenings, society weddings, and society funerals.

Young Maurice, born in 1860, was exiled from that aristocratic eden at the age of sixteen, when his father pulled him abruptly from school and sent him out to India. That—along with the fact that he apparently never received more than a pittance of the family fortune—are enough to hint at a dark cloud of impropriety hanging over him already in adolescence.

His first post in the East was a cushy one, surely arranged via his highly placed connections: as a very junior officer serving aboard the state yacht of the current viceroy of India, the Earl of Lytton. Within a few years, however, his maritime career came to an abrupt end, and—just as his father had expelled him from Britain—Lord Lytton exiled him to the remotest reaches of his viceregal domain. A note in his official service record described the removal as "temporary." It was not. Until the dawn of the next century, Portman would hold, without promotion or significant pay raise, the worst job in the worst place in the British Empire: Officer in Charge of the Andamanese.

Yet the job and the place would come to obsess—even to possess—him. Within the small compass of that remote archipelago, Portman would find the same fierce ardor for discovery that also drove such men as Burton, Speke, Livingstone, and Shackleton on their journeys into the hearts of distant continents.

He was still a teenager when he stepped onto the wharf at Port Blair early in 1879. The settlement by then had rooted itself firmly in the soil of Great Andaman. A Chief Commissioner reigned in a certain degree of state from an intimidating villa atop Mount Harriet, its entry hall festooned in baronial fashion with arrays of Andamanese bows, spears, and arrows, hung in elaborate geometrical patterns above clusters of more businesslike British service revolvers. Apart from this officer and a small cadre of subordinates and their wives, the European population comprised two companies of troops and a few other military men. Supported by several hundred Indian sepoys and a thousand or so Sikh policemen, they kept watch over some ten thousand convicts from the mainland, most of them serving life sentences at hard labor. Often, those life sentences did not last very long.

The little place ran as tightly as a brass chronometer. The white linen uniforms were pressed, the pith helmets brushed and buffed. Britons of any rank traveled about the place in sedan chairs like Turkish pashas, each borne on the shoulders of four sturdy convicts. In an endless stream of official communiqués, every rupee was accounted for, every prisoner was numbered, every pound of coconut oil and foot of lumber wrung from forced labor was tallied in neat columns. Discipline had grown only stricter since a lamentable tragedy seven years earlier, when the late viceroy, the Sixth Earl of Mayo, had visited Port Blair on an inspection tour. "We are all British gentleman engaged in the magnificent work of governing an inferior race," Lord Mayo had once said, referring to the natives of India. On his last evening in the Andamans, as he and Lady Mayo stopped at the quayside to admire the sunset, a member of that "inferior" race—namely, a Pathan convict—leapt out of the twilight and slashed him to death with a knife. After that incident, no more viceroys inspected Port Blair.

Portman's business, almost alone of his fellow Britons', was not with the convicts. His job, as officer in charge of the Andamanese, was to oversee the orphanage and Andaman

Homes, look to the welfare of the friendly islanders, pacify the unfriendly ones, and generally keep a sharp eye on things.

None of the penal colony's sun-browned and barrel-chested senior officers could have expected much of Portman in those early days. He must have appeared to them almost a caricature of the chinless aristocrat: a weedy, moody, slightly stooped young man, afflicted with what were then called "artistic tendencies." (He had brought his cherished violin with him to Port Blair.) Soon, however, he revealed a streak of unexpected grit. One day, as Portman trundled past a convict chain gang in his sedan chair, a prisoner lashed out at him suddenly with a heavy tool, knocking him senseless with a blow to the head. He was only saved from death by the quick intervention of the convict overseer.

Surprisingly, young Portman bore his severe wound with the pluck of a true Englishman, and was promptly out of sickbed and back about his work. The assailant, Convict #21545, was duly tried and hanged ten days later, while the prisoner who saved Portman's life was released from the penal colony with a full pardon for his crimes.

Such fortitude served him well as he stepped into his new job. It took no especially sharp eye to see that the islanders were in a dreadful state. Measles and syphilis epidemics were still ravaging the tribes of Great Andaman. Periodically, a group of sad-eyed natives would appear on the edge of a settlement, bearing an important tribal elder in the last stages of illness—blind, spasmodic, hallucinating—in the vain hope that the white men's medicine could save him. No one knew exactly how many of the other Andamanese were dying in the far-flung settlements—but enough that the authorities opened an orphanage for children with no relatives left to care for them.

Little effort was made to isolate the sick. Once, Portman saw a young native covered in oozing smallpox pustules, wandering about disoriented near the central Andaman Home. None of the British overseers had taken any steps to treat him, or to keep him from infecting others.

The newly appointed Officer in Charge could not have gleaned much of this situation from sitting down to read the official dossiers and communiqués penned by his predecessors. Although we know from many other sources that the indigenous inhabitants of Great Andaman—apart from the still isolated Jarawa—were on a rapid slide toward extinction, the monthly and yearly reports to Calcutta remained stubbornly, almost surreally, upbeat. They focused on the number of natives in the Homes, on how many rupees' worth of blankets and thatching leaves they had produced, and on how many rupees had been saved by economizing on their care. When they mentioned the epidemics, they usually noted briskly that the natives' health was improving, or at least their mortality was dropping. (None seemed to consider that perhaps there were fewer and fewer of them left to die.)

The true state of things became fully evident when Portman began to venture into remoter parts of the archipelago. Shortly after his arrival, he went on a short voyage with the Chief Commissioner to Port Campbell, a bay on Great Andaman's western coast. This was one of the most beautiful inlets in the archipelago: a long, limpid sheet of water, glassy as a tidal pool. The men intended to visit an Andamanese village tucked among the palm trees at the far end, the principal seat of a substantial tribe that customarily welcomed visitors—native or white—with exuberant dances and ceremonial pomp. Instead, they found the place uninhabited. All along the coast it was the same: at settlement after settlement, the huts and lean-tos had been reduced to collapsed heaps of bamboo and palm fronds, bleaching under the tropical sun.

Gradually, Portman would piece together what had happened. The culprit had not been a single epidemic, but rather one illness upon another. The really devastating chain of fatalities had been set off by syphilis some seven or eight years earlier. Apparently, the chief petty officer overseeing the central Andaman Home on Ross Island—a convict rewarded with that post for his good behavior—had infected many of the female inmates there. ("The married women were far from chaste," Portman explained, "and were willing to yield themselves to the convicts for small rewards and, of course, when threatened.") Some of these women went back to the jungle, where they spread the disease quickly, not just through their "immorality"—Andamanese custom afforded unmarried men and women a degree of sexual freedom unthinkable to well-bred Britons—but from more casual skin-to-skin contact, such as when members of an entire family or even village slept huddled together naked, a frequent practice. All the infants in a village might be infected by the custom of passing them from woman to woman for nursing. Syphilis killed some and left many others sick and enfeebled. Some might have been saved by European medicine, or at least kept from infecting others, but few wanted to come into Port Blair and risk dying in quarantine, separated from their families. Portman's predecessor had ultimately chosen to emphasize the "good deterrent effect" that this sexually transmitted scourge had upon the survivors: witnessing its awful devastation had been a "wholesome" warning against sexual promiscuity.

Ophthalmia had come next. Many Andamanese were left

wholly or partially blind—an especially crippling condition for people who lived on the fish they could catch in the lagoons and the fruit they could gather in the jungle. Some were further disabled by the alcoholism that had become endemic among them, fueled by the Englishmen's practice of dispensing free rum daily at the Andaman Homes as an enticement for the inmates to remain there.

And then measles struck. With no immunity to the disease, with their systems already sapped by the other illnesses and hardships, and with their families and villages in disarray, the natives mustered little resistance. Those who came to the Andaman Homes seeking succor often ended up fleeing from the harsh conditions there, spreading infection to villages far from the English settlement and the convict camps. Tribes remoter still were devastated by the colonizers' habit of kidnapping islanders from newly contacted groups, bringing them back to Port Blair—and then, when the captives grew ill, returning them to their homes.

Just at this moment, Portman decided to visit North Sentinel Island. He would also be responsible for the only instance when natives of North Sentinel are documented to have visited the world beyond it.

WHAT DREW PORTMAN was ultimately the same thing that would much later draw John Chau, T. N. Pandit, and me: it was, in his own words, still terra incognita. By 1879, North Sentinel seemed like the last truly unexplored island within reach, and the last place for a true first encounter with another human tribe, in all its savage innocence. A decade or two earlier, such opportunities had abounded throughout the Andamans. Now this remained the one inhabited place that the Englishmen had not penetrated. Portman had heard the tales of long-haired wild men who killed shipwrecked sailors without mercy. But such picturesque savages sounded far more alluring than the diseased, defeated inmates of the Andaman Homes.

Moreover, the new young Officer in Charge of the Andamanese had decided that his work was not just to superintend the natives, but to understand them.

Portman liked the islanders; he seems, indeed, to have been far more comfortable among them than among his own stubbornly insular colonial countrymen. He began filling notebooks with observations of the natives' culture, music, crafts, huts, food, tattoos. He scribbled notes in the margins of previous observers' books and articles, pointing out every error, whether minor or major. (No, the Andamanese did not eat bee larvae "to correct constipation," but rather simply because they enjoyed the taste. No, they did not paint their newborn infants with "red ochre," but rather with white clay. No, they were not immune to scurvy.)

He had also set about to learn the native tongues, which were pleasantly quick and lilting and, to most of the colonizers, absolutely unintelligible. Few other Englishmen had attempted to master them, and fewer still attained any degree of success—to be fair, the various Andamanese tribes spoke a baffling thicket of dialects—and had instead expected the islanders themselves (despite their supposed intellectual deficiencies) to familiarize themselves with both their own tongue and that of the Hindu sepoys. But Portman possessed a clever youth's quickness with languages—back on the mainland, he had picked up Hindustani within a year or two—combined with the methodical patience of a man beyond his years.

Maurice Vidal Portman, Officer in Charge of the Andamanese, surrounded by Andaman Islanders, c. 1884. The six men wearing hats and white surplices with crosses are probably members of a Masonic order that Portman is known to have brought to the Andamans in the early 1880s. (See page 246.)

He was soon chitchatting passably with natives of Great Andaman; not long after that, he undertook to review and revise such lexicons of the language as previous administrators had attempted to compile. Their efforts had been laughably deficient. They had misheard words and mangled syntax. Perusing a certain Major Tickell's vocabulary list of one hundred and nine Andamanese words and phrases, Portman found that only eight had been rendered correctly. Partly this was due to the natives' habit of deliberately misleading their questioners. When Major Tickell pointed to a flower and asked what they called it, they gave him the word for *shit*. He dutifully copied this into his notebook.

Scorning such errors, Portman began to assemble a lexicon of his own, adding to it as he encountered members of different tribes. He recorded each expression not just in one Andamanese dialect, but four or five, focusing especially on scripted dialogue that would be useful to his fellow Britons. Phrasebooks can often be inadvertently revealing texts, and Portman's was no exception. His lexicon tells us a great deal—far more, indeed, than any official report to Calcutta or London—about the conduct of imperial emissaries as they ventured into distant reaches of the island chain.

That man must be washed.
You must not sit here.
You will make everything dirty.
Take care, it is very heavy.
Some convicts have escaped, you must search for them.
Come and pick these ants off my clothes.
Get me that orchid.
Get me some oysters.

Dive for that coral.

Take me to your village.

This village is very dirty.

Get a broom and clean this hut.

Have the people here been doing anything wrong?

How did this woman become blind?

How is this man so covered with sores?

How is his face so swollen?

Why did you let a syphilitic woman tattoo him?

Where are all the women?

There are no children here.

PORTMAN WAS CERTAIN that he could learn far more from the archipelago's remote tribes than from those whose culture, customs, and language were already corrupted by contact with European settlers and Indian convicts. At North Sentinel, he thought, he could study the natives in their virgin habitat.

He made his first, brief attempt on the same trip as the visit to Port Campbell. He and the Chief Commissioner anchored off the island's surrounding reef, were rowed across the lagoon in the steamer's launch, and landed on the beach without incident. Portman noticed immediately that it was different from any other place he had visited in the Andamans. North Sentinel felt almost like a Pacific atoll that had come unmoored and drifted into the Indian Ocean: not stone or sand, but coral. Everywhere were bleaching chunks of ancient reef: eroded boulders awash in vegetation, the accreted exoskeletons of long-dead living things. Coral shards made walking painful, even in his sturdy boots.

He saw no living people that time, on his first tentative

venture into the Sentinelese forest. There had been no long-haired warriors waiting to spear them on the beach, and apparently none waiting in ambush, either. Portman and the Chief Commissioner could tell that the forest paths had been worn down by human feet, and they even spotted several small villages of lean-to huts. All were abandoned. For the first time, he used what would become a habitual word for the natives here: *timid*.

What left the strongest impression on him that day was the trees. The jungle on North Sentinel, unlike the impenetrable green tangle on Great Andaman and most of the outlying islands, was open in many places, almost parklike: the trees were so immense that no lesser growth could compete with them for light and sustenance. The Englishmen made their way warily through stands of padauk and groves of gnarled mahuas, as unseen birds and insects chorused on all sides. The largest species here had no homely common names, just grandiose Latin ones conferred by European naturalists. *Bombax malabaricum*, portentous as a witch's curse, spread its monstrous buttress roots like tentacles, clutching the earth in a death grip. On one of his visits to North Sentinel, possibly that one, Portman found the hunched skeleton of an old man hidden in a basket among the roots, chrysalis-like in its manmade cocoon.

These pale, living columns were more ancient than his own home island's Elizabethan oaks, straighter and statelier than the avenues in Hyde Park, higher than the church spires of London. His grandfather's estate in Dorsetshire was famous for its lordly plane trees: the tallest in Europe, some people said. North Sentinel's giants dwarfed them. How could an island this small seem somehow bigger than England?

The explorers retreated quickly from their brief foray,

determined to come back for a more thorough and methodical expedition. Portman wanted to meet elusive Sentinelese face to face, to become the first white man they knew.

He returned a few weeks later, this time in the surveying schooner *Constance*. He traveled, as he would later write in his monthly report, "with the intention of making friends with the inhabitants." Still nervous about native arrows, Portman brought a large party of armed men with him, a decision that he would later confess had been a mistake. Sweating and swearing as they made their cumbersome way through the jungle, with sabres rattling and cartridge-boxes swinging, the officers and soldiers managed to frighten off any Sentinelese. As soon as these intruders came within earshot, the natives retreated into the darkest corners of the forest, elusive as owls. A few times, Portman got close enough to discern what he would describe as their "peculiarly idiotic expression of countenance, and manner of behaving." (Could it be that this was how he perceived their understandable terror?)

One day, in Portman's words, "after much trouble some children were caught, loaded with presents, and then let loose." (His use of the passive voice leaves readers to guess at the exact nature of the "trouble," and the exact means by which the young islanders "were caught.") As soon as the children were out of their captors' grip, they dropped the gifts—which, based on other British dealings with the natives, probably included things like scrap iron, tobacco, looking-glasses, and brightly colored cloth—and fled for their lives. The Englishmen did manage to secure some gifts for themselves: from the hastily evacuated Sentinelese huts, they gathered bows, arrows, baskets, ancestral bones, and other artifacts that Portman thought might prove useful to researchers.

"Bullet wood trees, North Sentinel Island,"
photograph by Maurice Vidal Portman, c. 1894.

*"Spies hiding in the buttressed trees, North Sentinel Island," c. 1894.
This photograph is part of a series for which Portman brought some
indigenous men from another island to North Sentinel and had them
pose in the jungle pretending to be Sentinelese hunters. They were probably members of the Onge tribe of Little Andaman.*

Finally, after nearly two weeks tromping to and fro around the little island, Portman and his men managed to capture a few more stragglers. They had begun hunting more stealthily, fanning out through the forest in a rough crescent, like Highland beaters on a shooting day flushing pheasants from the heather. One day they kidnapped three more children, this time prudently sending them back to the *Constance* right away. Soon after, when Portman and an English officer were at the center of the line, they found themselves suddenly face-to-face with an old man, an old woman, and a small child. The man drew his bow and was about to loose the arrow when Portman's convict orderly leapt onto the assailant's back. The three natives were taken unhurt back to the schooner.

Even Portman himself later admitted that his strenuous efforts to befriend the Sentinelese had not been very successful, and in fact had not done anything but "increase their general terror of, and hostility to, all comers." Still, in the interest of science, the captives were kept aboard the *Constance* and taken back to Port Blair for observation.

Unfortunately, the six Sentinelese did not thrive there. Portman later blamed "the new style of food, and the excitement they must have been in." This diagnosis was surely insufficient. All six grew rapidly sicker. The old man and his wife died. The ailing children were sent back to their island, laden with presents. What alien microbes they may also have borne on that homeward journey can only be guessed.

THE FOLLOWING YEAR, back in London, the young explorer received an extraordinary honor. Home from the Andamans on temporary sick leave, the prodigal Portman, just twenty-one years old, was invited to address the august members of the Royal Asiatic Society at its headquarters in Piccadilly. This upstart sprig, a boy whose formal education had ended at sixteen, now stood before a body whose ranks included eminent professors and members of parliament; assorted major generals, high commissioners, and at least one former prime minister.

Portman brought with him an array of artifacts that he had collected in the Andamans—including several human jawbones from North Sentinel Island. He told the assemblage about his experiences venturing into remote areas of the archipelago, spending time among the primitives, and observing their ways of life. While admitting that "to a casual observer they appear repulsive," Portman assured his audience that "it is only after long association that one can appreciate their good qualities. I was on very friendly terms with them, and always found them affectionate, trustworthy, and kind." He hastened to add, however: "I regret to say that the general tone of their morals is far from being correct."

Science was interested in the Andamanese. Since the publication of Darwin's *On the Origin of Species* in 1859, this tiny human population—thought by Europeans to represent the most primitive and animalistic branch in our entire species—had played an outsize role in debates about the theory of evolution. Most scholars thought their existence supported Darwin's argument. After all, if *Homo sapiens* had indeed evolved from apes, it stood to reason that certain branches of the species had remained more apelike than others.

Over a decade later, in his 1871 book *The Descent of Man*, the great thinker himself referred to "the low and degraded inhabitants of the Andaman Islands." Specifically, Darwin noted their apparent tendency to die as soon as they were removed from their native home, in contrast to members of "the civilised races." Darwin noted that "many of the wilder races of man" shared this characteristic with the Andamanese, as did chimpanzees, gorillas, and orangutans, which rarely survived long in European zoos. Here was proof that different types of human beings, like other animals, evolved differently in response to different habitats, and traits that were favorable in one enviroment might doom them in another. (Darwin failed to acknowledge the cruel fact that the "degraded" people had probably succumbed to diseases carried by the "civilised" ones.)

Meanwhile, Darwin's collaborator and critic Alfred Russel Wallace used the Andamanese in an 1869 article to support a different hypothesis. He had read rosy reports from Port Blair about the progress toward civilization that these aborigines—"the lowest savages"—were making under their careful tutelage at the Andaman Homes. This convinced Wallace that despite countless millennia living primitive lives that would only demand an intellect "a little superior to that of an ape," the typical Andamanese possessed a brain "very little inferior to that of the average members of our learned societies." How, he argued, could evolution alone have bestowed the same intellectual capacity on all human races, even those that lived like wild animals? Instead, such universally innate human intelligence could only have been granted by a higher power. The Andamanese, then, were proof of God's existence. (In his copy of Wallace's article, Darwin wrote "No" next to this passage, underlined the word three times, and added a thicket of exclamation points.)

The fact that none of these theorists had ever met an actual Andamanese person did not deter them in the slightest. The eminent Professor William Henry Flower, director of London's Natural History Museum, declared that he "had never had the privilege of seeing an Andaman islander alive, but [I have] examined many of their bones and skulls." It was "most remarkable," he said, that some parts of their archipelago appeared to be "as isolated from the civilised world as any region could be. . . . These islands are therefore of great interest to anthropologists, and all information about the natives of them is of very great value."

The Andamanese continued to interest European racial theorists well into the twentieth century. Baron Egon Rudolf Ernst Adolf Hans Dubslaff von Eickstedt, a monocle-wearing German anthropologist whose work on "racial hygiene and eugenics" influenced the Nazis, visited the archipelago in the 1920s. Afterward, in his *Racial History of Mankind*, he characterized the Andamanese as humans of a "primitive chimpanzoid type."

These scientists' fascination—and their racism—filtered into popular culture. In Arthur Conan Doyle's 1890 novel *The Sign of the Four*, Sherlock Holmes investigates a series of murders in which a mysterious assailant skulks about London with a blowgun, killing men with poisoned darts and then disappearing into the shadows. It turns out that the murderer is a savage pygmy from the Andamans named Tonga, brought to the city by an English ex-convict who had escaped from the penal colony. At the climax of the book, the two malefactors slip out of London in a small steamboat under cover of darkness, and Holmes and Watson pursue them down the Thames in a thrilling high-speed chase. Watson, the narrator, describes the Andaman Islander suddenly appearing in the stern of the fleeing boat, "a little black man—the smallest I have ever seen—with a great, misshapen head and a shock of tangled, dishevelled hair":

Holmes had already drawn his revolver, and I whipped out mine at the sight of this savage, distorted creature. He was wrapped in some sort of dark ulster or blanket, which left only his face exposed; but that face was enough to give a man a sleepless night. Never have I seen features so deeply marked with all bestiality and cruelty. His small eyes glowed and burned with a sombre light, and his thick lips were writhed back from his teeth, which grinned and chattered at us with a half animal fury.

"Fire if he raises his hand," said Holmes, quietly. We were within a boat's-length by this time, and almost within touch of our quarry. I can see the two of them now as they stood, the white man with his legs far apart, shrieking out curses, and the unhallowed dwarf with his hideous face, and his strong yellow teeth gnashing at us in the light of our lantern.

It was well that we had so clear a view of him. Even as we looked he plucked out from under his covering a short, round piece of wood, like a school-ruler, and clapped it to his lips. Our pistols rang out together. He whirled round, threw up his arms, and with a kind of choking cough fell sideways into the stream. I caught one glimpse of his venomous, menacing eyes amid the white swirl of the waters.

Little matter that the real-life Andamanese did not use blow-guns and poison darts, nor did they have thick lips, small eyes, tangled hair, or misshapen heads. The "unhallowed dwarf" Tonga was the perfect foil to the suave, pale, cerebral Holmes. For Doyle, a black Andaman Islander was the photographic negative of a white Englishman. In all of his six dozen stories and novels about Sherlock Holmes, this is the only instance in which Doyle depicted his hero killing another human being.

FOR THE PAST few decades, Portman has been a figure of fascination to the very small circle of scholars who study Andamanese history. Part of his mystique has been that despite his voluminous scholarly writings and his prominent family, almost no record survived of his personal life. He left no wife or children, nor was there evidence that he ever had a romantic relationship with any man or woman. "Of all the Andamanese pioneers," one researcher wrote after many years of investigation, "Maurice Vidal Portman is by far the most fascinating, unapproachable, elusive, even mysterious."

At a certain level, his experiences in the Andamans are better documented than those of any other traveler. Throughout his twenty years in the archipelago, he produced a steady stream of official reports on his frequent travels among the islands. Portman's missives, compiled into crisp dossiers imprinted with the imperial coat of arms, duly made their way to the viceregal authorities in Calcutta, then to the India Office in London:

On the 22nd of November, the Chief Commissioner, I, and a large party of Andamanese left in the Indian Government Steamer "Kwangtong" to visit the Islands.

On the morning of the 23rd, we visited the North Centinel, left quantities of presents, but saw none of the inhabitants, although from the new huts, boats &c., which we saw, it was evident they were on the Island.

His buttoned-up dispatches told everything and revealed nothing: skirmishes, seashells, epidemics, and the deaths of entire villages were described with equal dispassion.

But in 2019, on a research visit to the rare book collection of the British Library in London, I came across something I had not expected to find. An entry in the online catalogue described an item that seemed only of marginal interest: *Journal of an unidentified medical officer in the Andaman Islands . . . 1883–1890*. Still, it was my last day in London, I'd already pored through all the books and manuscripts that I'd come to see, so I decided to take a look at this one.

The librarian at the circulation desk handed me the volume, its once elegant morocco-leather spine worn with age and use. Inside, the pages were filled with wildly scrawled notes in pencil. Turning the leaves carefully, growing accustomed bit by bit to the difficult handwriting, I gradually realized what I was holding: not a medical officer's journal, but rather Maurice Vidal Portman's very private diary.

Here were accounts of the same voyages he described in the brisk official reports—but as a kind of shadow text. Against library rules, I sneaked pictures of the pages with my phone, and over the coming months I would spend many hours poring over them, trying to make sense of the misshapen cursive, the private abbreviations, the coded language, and the peculiar vocabulary of Victorian India: *junglies*, *tiffin*, *muggra*. And they included certain details that he would certainly never have shared with his superiors. This parallel narrative eventually immersed me in a kind of dreamscape of science, violence, sex, drugs, and power. Like so much else about the Andaman Islands, it seemed to exist in a very narrow space between dream and nightmare, method and madness.

Portman's courage and resourcefulness were undeniable. He usually traveled in a small government steamer unaccompanied by any other Europeans, but instead with a retinue of convict servants and what he called *junglies*, or "tame" Andamanese from tribes that had made truce with their colonizers. Any of these companions, he must have known, could have ended his life at any moment with a hard shove from the boat's afterdeck or the swift strike of a belaying pin. He landed, often alone, on unknown shores where unfamiliar tribes lurked in the forests. Several times, he faced native arrows with apparent bravery that bordered on nonchalance. At all times he seemed to maintain an iron grip on those who surrounded him, and almost on the vagaries of fate itself.

His missions were often dangerous ones. One month he might be sent in pursuit of escaped convicts, another on a punitive expedition against hostile Andamanese who had murdered a colonial policeman. His superiors usually made their instructions very clear: *Orders being to catch or shoot.*

Notwithstanding his youth—he was still in his early-to-mid-twenties—and his lack of any university education, Portman investigated his surroundings with the keen eye of a linguist, a naturalist, and an anthropologist. Exploring beaches, reefs, and bluffs, he carefully catalogued species of animals and types of minerals that he encountered there. He seemed curious about almost everything, indeed, except his fellow Englishmen. The diaries include no description whatsoever of those who were his occasional traveling comrades, and at each return to Port Blair, his entries abruptly stop. The busy doings of the colony seemingly held no attraction. Nor do the Indian convicts appear as anything but sporadic bit players in his narratives.

Yet a disturbing portrait gradually emerges of his own character—and of the inner life of a very peculiar young man. Like other outsiders drawn to North Sentinel, and to the Andamans generally, he could often seem compulsive, even obsessive.

Repeatedly, he returned to North Sentinel. Repeatedly, he tried to capture some of the natives—and always, with the lone exception of his first visit, he failed. Once, a few days after Christmas in 1886, Portman ventured to the island with a small party of Andamanese and a few Europeans. This time he had higher hopes than usual, since his native companions included several members of the Onge tribe from Little Andaman Island, believed to be culturally similar to the Sentinelese. He anchored the steamer off the island's southeastern shore. Walking about on the beach, at the edge of the jungle, he found only empty huts. The Onge, "quite fearless," ventured deep into the forest. On returning, "they reported that they found them but to their astonishment discovered they spoke a different language and were by no means friendly."

Portman carefully interrogated members of the "friendly" tribes to glean whatever hearsay he could gather about North Sentinel. In one journal entry, he carefully noted the word that the Onge used for the island: *Chie táquĕqué*. This is the only instance when a native name for North Sentinel has ever been recorded by an outsider; it is unclear whether the term was (and perhaps still is) the one that the Sentinelese use for their homeland, or simply one current among the inhabitants of Little Andaman. The Onge also told him that the Sentinelese were known now and then to visit tribes on other outlying islands south of Great Andaman. The next sentence in Portman's diary made me gasp with surprise: "They add that I once attacked and shot them." Frustratingly, Portman did not clarify what incident this statement might have referred to, nor how the Onge might have learned of it.

To say that Portman was mercurial is an understatement.

His energetic work was interrupted by bouts of languor: whole days spent napping, reading, and strolling aimlessly on the beach: "Slept until tiffin. . . . After tiffin played the fiddle till tea." And for all his dedication to the Empire, for all his fascination with his exotic surroundings, he dreamed frequently of home.

More specifically, he dreamed of a life almost as contrary to his Andaman adventures as can be imagined, except for the astonishing breadth of expertise he planned to acquire.

The following are about my plans for the future:

> *If my father dies before I arrive home, or soon after, to get all my lecturing, visiting etc. over, and join the Royal College of Music at the Michelmas term. Study there for five years at least, and learn the entire theory of music thoroughly, also the Piano, Organ, Harp, Violin, Viola, Violoncello, Double Bass, and Flute. Then settle down somewhere in the SW of England to an organistship (good organ) and do music, and gardening.*

Sometimes, in his narrow berth aboard the steamer, Portman imagined a reconciliation with his grandfather and luxurious lodgings at 5 Prince's Gate, the old viscount's London mansion.

As I read through Portman's diary entries, I was surprised at how much time he found to practice on his violin. Once, on an expedition to remote Little Andaman, he wrote of playing Schubert's "Rosamunde Overture." In my carrel at the British Library, I downloaded the overture on my phone and listened, imagining him walking on the beach with the instrument

under his chin and his bow busy. The music haunted me for
the rest of my stay in London, and still often recurs when I
think of him. A few crashing chords yield suddenly to an elegant melodic line, wandering and melancholy. Then suddenly
the discordant storm crashes again, and all elegance is gone.

THE ANNALS OF the Age of Discovery are replete with moments
of intense physical connection. One of the most famous—tales
of which have inspired many generations of Western explorers—came in 1768, when the French explorer Louis Antoine
de Bougainville, midway through his voyage across the Pacific,
sighted a beautiful island rising out of the sea. After the mariners came ashore, the islanders spread the floors of their huts
with flowers and green leaves, and as native musicians, in the
captain's words, "sang an hymeneal song to the tune of their
flutes," crowds gathered and watched the Frenchmen and
island women lie down, two by two, to copulate on the leafy
beds. (It is not entirely clear in the captain's account whether
the women were entirely voluntary participants.) The place
already had a name—Tahiti—but Bougainville would call it La
Nouvelle Cythère, after the island where Aphrodite was born
from the waves.

Maurice Portman's diary contains moments of exuberant
connection with his Andamanese companions, moments when
he "skylarked" with them in the surf, joined in their ritual
sunset dances at dusk on the beach—which he referred to
ironically as "the cancan" or "quadrilles"—or entertained them
with a magic-lantern apparatus that he had brought along. He
seems to have regarded many of them with genuine fondness,
bestowing English names on his favorites. But whenever he

decided that the natives had misbehaved, he responded with violence, which he described with eerie dispassion:

> *Gave Mark, Bill, and Owen 12 stripes each. Bill screamed.*
> *   Others took it quietly.*
> *Thrashed the boy.*
> *Came on board and thrashed the junglies.*
> *Thrashed Owen and Bill pretty severely.*
> *Had to beat David.*
> *One convict's arm badly swollen where I hit him yesterday.*

Portman's erotic life revealed itself quite explicitly the moment I opened the second volume of his diaries. There on the faded orange endpapers were a series of pencil sketches of penises, some of them carefully delineated, others in faintest outline. All of them were strangely disembodied, detached from any other human form.

Examining the entries, I also began noticing the way he ended many of his days:

> *To bed with Wologa.*
> *To sleep. Warm night. Bill.*
> *Slept well. Owen.*
> *To sleep early. Bill.*
> *Served out Chateau d'Yquem & to bed. Mark.*

Context suggests that "Chateau d'Yquem" was another of Portman's private jokes, and that the liquid he served out nightly (sometimes also dosing himself) was actually a tincture of opium. Perhaps this was why his Andamanese companions remained in his thrall.

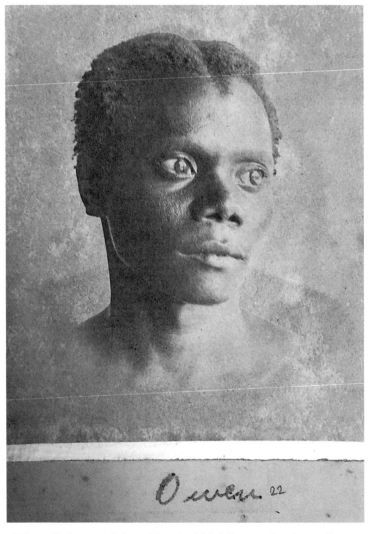

"Owen," photograph from Maurice Vidal Portman's private albums, c. 1890. The man's Andamanese name is unknown.

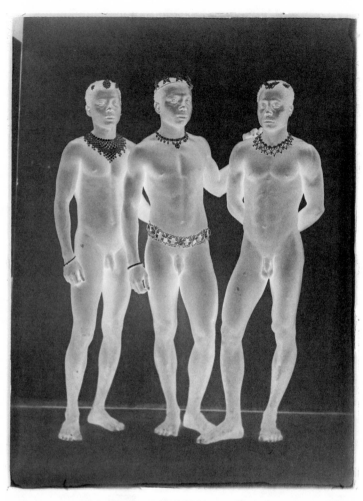

Portman captioned this image "Three athletes," c. 1890s. The young men, whom he identified elsewhere as "Daniel," "Hermes," and "The Cat-wára," posed in many of his photographs; all three are wearing fanciful ornaments that appear to be of Portman's own invention. He did not include this photograph in his official "Record of the Andamanese." The image above is from a glass plate negative in the British Museum.

Another apparent Portman code word for sex with the Andamanese was "talk" or "conversation." On one occasion he writes: "Lay and talked with Muggra, who declares I taught him, which is against evidence. They all will luckily admit nothing about others and are I hope to be depended on, though that is doubtful." Surely the thing that the native accused Portman of teaching him—and that the Englishman wished to keep secret—was something other than just lying down and having a chat. The entry also suggests that Portman was aware of, and took advantage of, the tolerant attitude toward same-sex relations prevalent in traditional Andamanese culture. (Unmentionable for the Victorians, this "prevalence of aberration" among the islanders was first described—and deplored—by an Italian anthropologist in the 1960s.)

Throughout his time in the Andamans, Portman suffered health complaints that he only vaguely described. He often wrote of aches, pains, and fevers. But one entry in his diary, from 1884, specifically mentions finding a "bubo" in his right groin. This could have been a symptom of tuberculosis. It could also have been a symptom of syphilis. In any case, it seems evident that he was spreading at least one of the diseases whose ravages he deplored in his official reports.

Portman's surviving diaries end in the autumn of 1890, halfway through his sojourn in the islands. Their latter pages record a trip to one of the remote areas in the northern reaches of Great Andaman—an area he had last explored in 1880, shortly after his arrival. On that first trip, he noted, fourteen canoe loads of Andamanese had come across the lagoon to greet him. Now, in the same spot, there were barely a dozen inhabitants left alive. He made inquiries among the survivors:

All people at Ulinwandoryé dead. Kobéda Kölé dead. They
then declared everyone was dead at every village I named.

And on the very last page of the journal, in a note about a
man he had slept with repeatedly a few years earlier, is one final
intimation of mortality:

Bill has Syph.

If Portman did continue keeping a diary, it seems likely that
the later volumes have not survived. But by this time, he had
shifted his attention to a new medium for recording his experiences among the Andamanese. This one would bestow eternal
life on the bodies of those people whom he loved and violated:
he was now traveling with a camera.

NEARLY ALL THE known photographs of North Sentinel have
been taken at a safe distance. From the sea's vantage, the island
is an abstraction. It is five stacked bands of color: the blue of
its lagoon, the yellow-white of its beach, the black of its jungle
understory, the deep green of its treetops, the broader blue of
boundless sky.

Of the island's interior, just a dozen black-and-white prints
exist. It is not easy to view them, as they have remained unpublished for the past hundred and twenty years and are tucked
away deep in the archives of the Anthropological Survey of
India, which in turn lie tucked away deep in a corner of the
Indian Museum in Kolkata, a crumbling relic of the Raj. The
only reason I knew of them was from an index, also unpublished, of Portman's photographs that a Swiss researcher

compiled many years ago. For months, I emailed and phoned seeking access, without any helpful reply. Finally, I decided to just show up.

Even after I arrived at the museum, the photographs seemed almost as inaccessible as the island itself. First, I had to bluff my way past the Indian soldiers guarding the entrance to a rear courtyard. The soldiers, in turn, summoned four members of the museum's staff, who were impressed that I'd come all the way from America to view some photographs, but told me to go away. At last I was handed off to a government functionary, who walked ten paces with me before handing me off to another functionary, who did the same thing. Four more functionaries later, I was in the office of the director of the Anthropological Survey, a courtly man with a Cambridge PhD and impeccable white hair. We sat drinking tea for an hour as I told him about my project. First, he professed to be unaware of the Portman photographs' existence. Then he told me that they were inaccessible to researchers. Finally, he asked me to go away and come back the next day with a letter of introduction. I would then be granted six hours to view twenty-six thick folio albums and copy a few of them for publication.

Those hours passed in a blur. Just as with the private diaries, I was seeing the Andamans through Portman's eyes, but this time even more literally. The experience was equally surreal. Here were men in spiked pith helmets and ladies with parasols, playing croquet before an audience of convicts and Andamanese. Here were Portman's spacious bungalow and garden at Port Blair, and the neat little white-bellied steam launch that carried him on his journeys around the archipelago.

Just a few of the photographs depicted the explorer himself, surrounded always by naked islanders. His face in these was

pale and blurred, a strange contrast to the ruthless specific-
ity with which he depicted the Andamanese. In one image, he
sits on a thronelike chair and some of the surrounding natives
wear white surplices with crosses on them, possibly denoting
their membership in a Masonic order that Portman established
during his sojourn in the archipelago.

The North Sentinel photographs were scattered in almost
random fashion among those other images. They seemed the
opposite of those already familiar beach photographs taken
in our own time. Rather than schematic bands of color, here
were tangled lines of black and white, intricate lattice works
of trunks and vines. Yet it is hard to imagine these images as
living jungle. The tree trunks manifest as pale, skeletal spec-
ters, and the light filtering through dense forest canopy seems
almost more arctic than tropical. Several of the photographs
depict native hunters in the North Sentinel forest, their small
bodies silhouetted against massive buttress roots. But these are
clearly posed, likely with Portman's "friendly" Andamanese
from other islands as his models. By his own admission, he
never managed to catch more than brief glimpses of the Sentinelese after his initial 1880 visit—certainly these interactions
never reached the point where the Sentinelese would stay still
in perfectly composed arrangements for a long-exposure camera. The images' very existence, however, attests to Portman's
fascination with these elusive people, and his wish to capture
them in one way or another.

THOSE PRINTS IN Kolkata were part of a much larger project.
Photography was initially just a hobby for Portman—as he once
described it, a way to pass the dreary hours during the mon-

soon season, when he was stuck on Great Andaman with little else to occupy him but gardening, reading books, and shooting pigeons. But it soon became something far more than an idle pastime. At some point in the late 1880s, Portman embarked on what would become his life's last great work. He contacted the British Museum and the imperial authorities with a plan: if the natives of the Andaman Islands were indeed fated to vanish from the world, he would use nineteenth-century technology to preserve them for posterity. All he required was a small government subsidy for this essential task. As he explained in a letter to one of his superiors: "Having regard to the fact that the Andamanese race will, in a few years, be extinct, [and] that there is no other photographic record of them . . . these photographs will be worth more in pounds than I am charging rupees." (In other words, their value would increase by a factor of at least fifteen.) In another letter, he warned that without his endeavors, "the Andamanese who are fast dying out will be left like the Tasmanians without any record."

Properly documenting the disappearing tribes—affixing them carefully in emulsion before they faded away completely, like negatives exposed too long to the sun—would require thousands of images. At a time when a single successful photograph, even under optimal circumstances, might require hours to produce, this would be a gargantuan labor. But Portman declared himself ready to undertake it.

The British Museum responded with enthusiasm. One of the institution's ethnographers wrote from London: "The series when complete on the scale you have proposed will be a most valuable monument of you and of the natives."

So Portman set about his work, to which he would devote the next twelve years. Why he did not instead dedicate himself to saving the flesh-and-blood Andamanese can only be con-jectured. Rather, he furnished his bungalow near Port Blair with a studio, a darkroom, and an electrical generator. He also turned it into a sort of unofficial Andaman Home where dozens of natives lived at a time—most of them men and boys under the age of twenty-six—while he cared for them and taught them European ways. They would soon become his primary subjects. Some also served as his studio assistants, holding light reflectors, mixing chemical solutions, and trundling his heavy and fragile box cameras when Portman brought his project to the outlying islands.

Many of Portman's photographs are, on a purely aesthetic level, extraordinarily beautiful. Surely his exquisite portraits of brooding young men—on whom he sometimes bestowed such un-Andamanese names as David, Daniel, and Hermes—can-not have been created for purely scientific purposes. Much less so a curious series of photographs in which he posed several of the most comely youths, naked except for a few fanciful, non-Andamanese adornments—tinselly stars, flowers, and butterflies—that he must have created himself. They stand before a blank white backdrop, angels flawless and floating, detached from earth.

Notwithstanding Portman's dire accounts of rampant sick-ness among the Andamanese, he chose only healthy sitters for his portraits. Yet a sense of doom pervades the pictures. In the hundreds of images, not one person smiles.

Eventually the British Museum gently nudged him. There had been whisperings of "indecency" about Portman's project, they warned. The ethnologists and anatomists dismissed this allegation but urged him to take a more scientific approach: instead of artful nudes, his photographs should portray the sub-

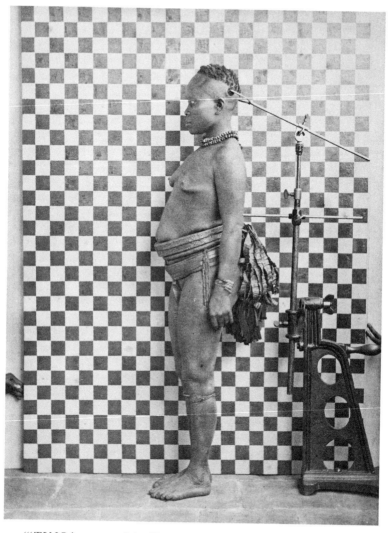

"'TIMO,' woman of the 'TA-KEDA' tribe; age about fifty years," c. 1894. A studio assistant's hand is visible at lower left.

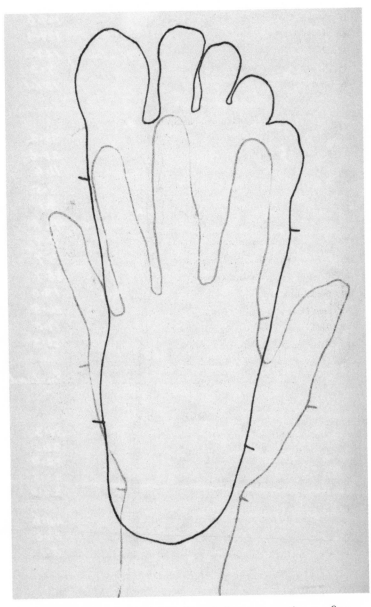

Tracing of the hand and foot of an Andamanese native, c. 1894.

Special Observations.

Name. KAUNMU. Nickname. DIU-TER-LÁRA. " He harpoons turtle " during the day ".

Quiet, good tempered disposition. Very intelligent, with considerable authority over his tribesmen. He is Chief of his tribe, and was one of the first to establish friendly relations between Europeans and the aborigines of the North Andaman.

Genitals fully developed. Married once. Has had one male child, now dead.

Teeth sound and regular.

Lobe of ear curved and detached. No trace of Darwin's point. The ears are not a pair.

No offensive smell from body or breath.

The first joint of the first finger off his right hand was bitten off by a fish.

Pulse 102 beats in a minute.

Breathing upper abdominal. 19 respirations in a minute.

Temperature in health 100°. Temperature of atmosphere being 84°.

Temperament sanguine.

Weight 118 lbs, 8 oz.

A page from Portman's record of Kaunmu,
an Andamanese man, 1894.

jects with clinical precision, both frontally and in profile, posed against a checkerboard backdrop to provide exact scale. They also provided him with a device called the Traveler's Anthropometer, a large steel caliper that could measure different parts of the natives' bodies with even greater precision.

SOON PORTMAN WAS not just photographing the Andamanese, not just measuring them, but also inspecting and describing every part of their bodies, taking their temperatures, counting their heartbeats, evaluating their personalities, remarking on those who seemed inordinately "lustful," even smelling them. He traced outlines of their hands and feet on pre-printed forms, where he also recorded every detail of possible value to science. He left traces of autobiography as well. Here is how he described Woichela, one of the young men who accompanied him on his expeditions:

> *Exceptionally plucky and brave. (Allowed me to fire at a small pot on his head, with an iron-pointed arrow.) Very good-tempered. Breath sweet. Not very lustful. Penis unusually large. Both testes well-formed. Is of average strength. Very obedient. All senses normal. Intelligent. truthful. Affectionate.*

As if these labors were insufficient, Portman also began writing a book. Published in 1899, his two-volume *History of Our Relations with the Andamanese* runs to almost nine hundred dense pages and details every significant interaction of Europeans with the native tribes for which he could find any record. He promised the British Museum additional volumes on Andamanese culture, language, and artifacts, plus dozens

ADAM GOODHEART · 179

more albums of photographs. He promised that "a complete record in imperishable Platinotype will be made of the Andaman Islander in every action of his life."

Strangely, Portman seems at last to have given up on North Sentinel. On page 764 of his magnum opus, he recommended to the colonial authorities that as soon as its inhabitants could be "tamed," the island should be converted into a coconut plantation, reversing a suggestion he had made several years earlier that it should become a place of "isolation" to which British authorities could eventually exile any surviving members of the Jarawa and other hostile tribes.

And then Portman's work ceased. On January 4, 1900—a few days into the twentieth century—he went on administrative leave. The voluminous official reports offer only a single line of unsatisfactory explanation: "Mr Portman's health completely broke down during the year and he was obliged to retire from the service of Government." As suddenly and mysteriously as he had left England for India more than two decades before, he left the islands where he had spent his entire life, never to return. He soon slipped into obscurity. A decade later, a traveler to the islands spoke with some natives who had lived with him and summarized her findings thus: "He had made pets of the Andamanese, and given them bicycles and champagne, relieved by occasional beatings."

Portman lived for another thirty-five years and, as far as can be discovered, never wrote another page about the Andaman Islands or their native inhabitants. The final paragraph of his 1899 book—written with a characteristic blend of poignancy and detachment—would appear to be his last word on the subject:

So long as they were left to themselves and not in any way interfered with by outside influences, or their customs, food, etc., altered, they would continue to live; but when we came amongst them and admitted the air of the outside world, with consequent changes, to suit our necessities, not theirs, they lost their vitality, which was wholly dependent on being untouched, and the end of the race came.

IN ADDITION TO its set of Portman's photographs, the British Museum possesses a collection that I didn't know about until I recently visited there. As I turned the album pages, the photography curator asked me casually, "Did you want to look at Portman's original negatives?"

A few minutes later, he wheeled out several library carts laden with ancient, dampstained wooden boxes, perhaps the same ones in which Portman had shipped them to the museum a century ago. Each bore faint pencil markings: GESTURES. SMOKING, EATING, DRINKING. FULL FIGURE PORTRAITS. Inside were hundreds of large-format glass plates.

Gingerly, I carried them one by one across the room to a flickering light table. These artifacts did not simply *portray* Portman's Andamanese sitters. The glass negatives had actually faced those long-dead men, women, and children, had witnessed their nakedness and directly captured their bodies' reflected light. The ephemeral moments trapped in their silver crystals might be the only surviving earthly traces of those vanished lives.

Lifting each fragile sheet was terrifying. I felt as if I were holding in my hands a still-beating heart.

I left a little while later, crossed the museum's courtyard, and emerged into central London on a sunlit winter afternoon. Throngs moved all around me: Europeans, Asians, Africans. Walking, chatting, eating, living. I thought about the vastness of this old imperial capital, about the millions of people who had dwelled here through the centuries, and about the billions of others who lived now in cities all over the world. I thought of Tonga's tiny body, bedded in the dark mud of the Thames. The enormous scale of our species' history surely reduced to insignificance the fates of a few hundred human beings on the far side of the planet.

Then I remembered those beautiful, doomed faces, and the busy streets of London were blurring with my tears.

IV

Third Journey

2020

Looking for cell service, Little Andaman Island,
January 2020.

One thing I learned for certain: man was not made to be alone.

—JOHN ALLEN CHAU,
"The End of the Trail," blog entry,
January 5, 2015

For now they knew that they had truly come to the beginning of the End of the World.

—C. S. LEWIS,
The Voyage of the Dawn Treader (1952)

Now I can hold the island between my fingertips: glowing, greener than I remember, the encircling sea a deeper blue.

Our plane is hurtling through the small hours of the night, somewhere in the dubious in-between time of international air travel. I'm on an Air Emirates flight: Washington-Dubai-Delhi; I'll then fly over to Kolkata before heading onward to Port Blair. The touch screen on the seatback in front of me is a luminous window opening onto a boundless realm of digital enticements, and has lured me in, even though I know I should be trying to sleep. Among the dozens of channels and hundreds of movies on offer, there is a feature called Global Explore. It traces our flight path across the continents, shows us what we are flying over—no need to raise the plastic blinds—and offers satellite views of the entire world.

I stroke the screen, right to left. The Persian Gulf sweeps past; the skirt of Asia; the jutting subcontinent. The Andamans appear, a scattering of green. Gently I touch the ocean around them and pull finger and thumb apart. Now I've found the place I'm looking for: a tiny, lonely square growing larger, like a single-celled life-form under a microscope, its beach a membranous wall. I touch again and again, as the island swells and resolves. I see the white surf in the lagoon, a dot that might be what's left of the Primrose, *and the forest* canopy dimpled with crowns of individual trees. The satellite view is at its inmost limit now, straining at an invisible barrier, just beyond the bounds of human scale. We can intrude no further here.

All around me in the airplane cabin, each passenger's pixelated square is telling its own private story, gleaming faintly on each intent face. Here, North Sentinel is still mine alone.

I turn my island, twirl it, then pull back. As it shrinks and shrinks again, the pale tectonic ridge beneath the Andamans reveals itself, like the submerged vertebrae of some prehistoric fish. The whole Indian Ocean fills the screen—but North Sentinel, astonishingly, still holds its own, dwindled to a single bright pixel.

Another pinch and even this is gone. Continents themselves fall away as the satellite view reaches its apex, where our planet's curving stratosphere shines like breakers on a reef. Now the whole globe spins at my touch, silhouetted against its final backdrop: a distant archipelago of stars.

Chapter 6

CALCUTTA WAS KOLKATA now, its old imperial nomenclature erased and reinscribed. When I'd last visited, two decades earlier, it felt as if the British, who'd shifted the Raj's capital to New Delhi in 1911, had only just packed up and left. Precarious Edwardian elevators rattled up and down the stairwells of downtown office buildings. Rickshaw-pullers and chai-wallahs crowded the side streets, crunching through heaps of discarded clay teacups that clogged the gutters. I visited a maharajah in his grimy palace, guarded by barefoot men with spears, where a monstrous statue of Victoria, the revered Queen-Empress—at least three times life-size, and balanced like a surfer on a teakwood froth of lions, unicorns, and Garters—occupied the place of honor. I'd wandered the city's streets for a long time in search of anywhere with internet access, which I'd finally found in an alleyway where a handwritten sign offered:

FORTUNE TELLER
COURIER
TELEX
EMAIL

Now, a few weeks into 2020, the rickshaw-pullers had vanished, and terracotta shards no longer paved the streets: tea

Maurice Vidal Portman with members of the Onge tribe in front of an indigenous hut, Little Andaman Island, c. 1890s.

vendors had switched finally to plastic. Nokia and Samsung signs seemed to have blossomed everywhere, and ads for gym memberships far outnumbered those for fortune tellers.

Before leaving on this trip, I'd planned to disconnect. I hadn't packed a laptop or tablet—only notebooks and pens—and seriously considered ditching my smartphone as well. I wanted to be attentive, wanted to turn outward, wanted not to lie awake in the small hours of the night, cupping that cold blue flame in my hands. After all, hadn't I made my way to the Andamans in my twenties without any digital help? Surely I could do it again. But my resolution crumbled pretty fast. Soon, I found myself staring at an an iPhone app as I navigated downtown Kolkata and checking every restaurant's Yelp review before eating there. I posted a snapshot on Facebook, guiltily deleted it, then posted it again.

Apparently the ferryboats still run to Port Blair once or twice a month, but this time I flew out on a two-hundred-passenger Air India jet crowded with tourists, one of ten daily flights from the mainland.

Still, I didn't expect the Andamans to be as changed as I found them, even before we disembarked. Beside our runway, an enormous new terminal was under construction, a tubular glass-and-steel structure that will accommodate thousands of passengers a day. Gone was the little frontier settlement that I remembered. Gone the muddy road that I'd wandered up from the ferry terminal in 1998, the roving cows and the paan-wallahs. Gone the sloping forests that once hemmed the town; gone the Government Telegraph Office; gone the harbor's wooden fishing boats with their narrow-beaked prows. It was almost impossible to walk anywhere now in the center of Port Blair, where the freshly asphalted roads had no sidewalks, and where crossing the complicated traffic circles required death-defying sprints through hurtling traffic. From the balcony of my hotel room, I could see the smear of yellow-gray smog streaking the sky.

The cell reception could be spotty, but it was there if you persisted. I spent a lot of time staring at my phone, waiting for the little bars to rise, hoping for a connection.

OVER THE PAST few years, most of the big travel magazines have published features on the Andamans. *Condé Nast Traveler*: "Why Your Next Island Getaway Should Be in India." ("One of the most untraveled corners of the world is finally opening up in a big way . . . [attracting] intrepid A-listers like Johnny Depp and Kate Winslet.") *Vogue*: "Why India's Andaman Islands Could Be the New Maldives." *Travel & Leisure* ranked the archipelago #1 on its 2021 list of "The Top Five Islands in Asia," with a score of 91.24 out of 100. (No matter that its photo showed an unrelated island five hundred miles away off the coast of Thailand.)

Nearly all the magazines and tourism websites mention the archipelago's native tribes: a crucial ingredient in the islands' distinctive charm. The local tourist industry is not unaware of this, either. A new beach resort and spa built by the Taj Hotels Group features seventy-two luxury bungalows—most with their own private swimming pools—that were purportedly designed to resemble Jarawa huts.

Travel promoters are also aware that for millions of potential visitors, the Andaman Islands' principal identity may be not as a premier vacation spot, but rather as the place where a young American was killed not long ago. They are quick to offer reassurance. North Sentinel Island, *Vogue* promised its readers, "is miles across the ocean from any tourist-friendly locales."

Not all Western travelers to the islands are the type who take their cues from *Vogue*. Over the past quarter-century, the Andamans have become a sought-after destination on the international surfing circuit. For many years, a tale has circulated about a boatload of top-ranked wave-hunters who somehow found their way into the North Sentinel lagoon. According to one secondhand account, the surfers, apparently unaware of the island's reputation, started riding the breakers, not noticing that a canoe full of spear-carrying Sentinelese was headed straight toward their charter boat. Thinking fast, the captain—or so the story goes—cranked up the vessel's sound system, which happened to be playing the opening keyboard riff of a French electronica track ("La Femme d'Argent," by a band called Air). The natives were supposedly so entranced by this alien music that they stopped paddling and just listened, giving the surfers time to escape unscathed. Like many stories about North Sentinel, this one is so strange—and so specific—that it might actually be true.

Islands in general have become a bit of a cultural fetish. There are entire Facebook groups devoted just to posting pictures of islands, whole magazines about islands. Tourism promoters talk about something called *island time*, a suspension of ordinary chronology. Vishvajit Pandya pointed out to me that the cultural meaning of islands has almost completely reversed itself over the past century or two. Once, they were thought of as pestilential, disease-ridden hellholes, homes for people with heads like dogs, suitable locations for penal colonies. In British colonial times, mainland Indians shuddered to think about being sent across the *kala pani*—the black water—to the Andamans. Now they line up to take vacations there, surrounded by waters of the most enticing blue.

Perhaps that shift has to do with how we think about isolation. The word itself comes from the Latin word for island, *insula*, the one on Claudius Ptolemy's maps. The more we are connected, the more isolation entices us. Certain kinds of connection can start to feel a whole lot like isolation, that digital blue flame replacing the communal campfire.

Of course, islands, both real and imaginary, are also places of discovery—places where we encounter things, or people, that upend our whole understanding of the world: Thomas More's Utopians, Jonathan Swift's Lilliputians. Oddly enough, the most famous island ever to have been "found" is now lost: the one that a grateful Columbus, making landfall after his first Atlantic crossing, named San Salvador, the blessed Savior. Historians still debate which of a half-dozen places might be the one that he described, not very specifically, as "very big and very level and the trees very green, and many bodies of water, and a very big lake [probably a lagoon] in the middle . . . and the whole of it so green that it is a pleasure to gaze upon" and with trees "as green and leafy as those of Castile in the months of April and May." He emphasized *green* over and over: the color of promise, the color of Eden.

According to one early chronicler, King Ferdinand of Castile remarked of Columbus that instead of the title he held, *almirante*, the admiral, he should be called *admirans*, the one who marvels. This may have been the same occasion on which the king stood as godparent to the six Native Americans whom Columbus had kidnapped on San Salvador—and who, with that sprinkling of holy water, were "savages" and Eden-dwellers no more.

. . .

IT ISN'T JUST by staying in faux Jarawa huts that today's visitors commune with the alluringly exotic Andamanese tribes. Over the years since my initial encounter with the Jarawa, they have become a tourist attraction.

Beginning in the early 2000s, reports from the islands described excursions in which tourists drove up the Andaman Trunk Road—the old single-lane highway from Port Blair up into the Andamanese hinterlands. For decades, vehicles had traveled the road only with Bush Police protection, under threat of Jarawa attacks. But as word spread of the tribe's friendly contacts with the outside world, curiosity-seekers began to trickle in. Before long, buses were heading up the Trunk Road expressly so that tourists could—usually with the help of a bribe to police—stop to take pictures and videos of the equally curious Jarawa. Indian media condemned these encounters as "human safaris," but little was done to stop them. Soon, tribal people learned to pose and dance for the visitors in exchange for bananas or packets of potato chips. They started hitching rides in the passing cars, even on top of buses. Poachers who had been wary of entering the tribal area became bolder, despite periodic clashes with the natives. Dark rumors of sexual exploitation circulated in Port Blair.

What happened next was probably inevitable. Within a year of my visit to Tirur in 1998, an epidemic of measles—the same disease that had killed so many Andamanese in the nineteenth century—broke out among the Jarawa.

One day during my return trip to Port Blair, I happened to encounter Ratan Chandra Kar, the physician whom I had last seen at Kadamtala two decades earlier. It turned out that he had continued working with the Jarawa for a full twelve years after our first meeting. Public health authorities had set him up in a small rural clinic at the edge of the tribal reserve, with the express purpose of providing medical care to the tribe. Kar told me that with the aid of anti-inflammatory drugs and antibiotics, he had managed to prevent any measles cases he treated from becoming fatal. He conceded, however, that no one could tell how many deaths there had been among Jarawa in remoter areas who had not come out of the forest.

Kar gradually ventured deep into the jungle, gaining substantial knowledge of the Jarawa language and culture. "We tried to discover them, and they also tried to discover us," he said. "After five years with them, I was able to ask in their language, 'What do you think of civilized people?' They said that there is too much disease in the civilized world. So I asked them why they were coming out so much, and coming to the hospital. They said, 'We want to live in our country, but from time to time we want to come to you.'" Kar painted an optimistic picture of the Indians' interactions with the Jarawa during his time among them. They had taught him some of their traditional songs. He had taught the children to play soccer. A few of the boys even learned to head the ball rather well.

But then the doctor told me something truly surprising. I asked him what had become of Enmei, the Jarawa teenager I had met in 1998, dressed in his T-shirt and baseball cap. Perhaps he was a tribal leader now, an intermediary between his people and the outside world?

Instead, Kar told me, Enmei had returned to the forest. He had fallen in love with a Jarawa girl named Shyla, whose parents would not let them marry unless the young man gave up his strange new ways. He was seen only occasionally now, hunting with his bow and arrows, naked as before.

· · ·

OTHERS WHOM I met during my return to the Andamans also told unexpected stories.

Denis Giles publishes the only local "opposition" paper in the islands, the *Andaman Chronicle*. Its circulation is around eight hundred copies, and its office is a single room with a couple of cluttered desks and an old-fashioned printing press. Giles, a man in his forties, has a round, open face that makes him seem younger than his years.

India's national government, he told me, had begun paying attention to the indigenous Andamanese only after international human rights groups began sounding the alarm about the "human safaris." Its response had been inconsistent to the point of perversity. First, in 2002, India's Supreme Court had ordered the closing of the Andaman Trunk Road, a ruling celebrated by local activists and foreign human-rights groups—but which had been completely ignored by local authorities. Then the government appointed a special committee to investigate the Jarawa situation and recommend a course of action. After a year, the committee issued a four-hundred-page report that was full of interesting stories about the officials' various personal encounters with the picturesque tribesmen—but that contained almost no recommendations whatsoever. More recently, the Hindu nationalist government of Narendra Modi has shown little interest, if any. The prime minister briefly visited the islands, gave a speech in which he summarily renamed four islands that still bore British colonial toponyms, and departed without even mentioning the indigenous people.

Nonetheless, the situation started improving in the early 2010s, after tourists began posting YouTube videos of their encounters with the Jarawa, drawing outrage in foreign media over members of an isolated tribe being treated as exotic attractions. (One, which showed an Indian policeman ordering naked tribal women to dance for a group of visitors, sparked especially vehement denunciations.) Embarrassed, the Indian government finally clamped down—banning tour operators from offering trips into the tribal reserve and forbidding travelers on the Trunk Road from stopping their cars, from taking photos or videos, and from interacting in any way with Jarawa whom they might incidentally encounter. The Bush Police of former days have been given a new name and identity: Tribal Welfare Officers.

The Sentinelese, too, seemed safer than they once had been. Anthropologists and local officials made a few last forays to the nearby waters in the early 2000s, but the missions stopped over a decade ago. After John Chau's ill-fated visit, Giles and other activists worried that all of the international attention might lead others to brave the tribal people's arrows. It had not—and in fact, the Indian Navy now seemed to be patrolling the surrounding ocean more assiduously than before.

Giles and other local activists have teamed up with international groups to make sure that the increased protections are maintained. Ultimately, he is optimistic about the Andamanese tribes' future: "We are watching over them now with eyes and ears across the world."

But he also told me that he wasn't too worried about the Jarawa who are taking tentative steps toward living more like their Indian neighbors—wearing clothes, learning Hindi, and even sending their children to small "bicultural" schools that Indian authorities have created near the edge of the tribal reserve. Giles believes in induvidual freedom, he says. Some of the Jarawa want one thing; some want another. We must never forget that just like us, they each have their own personality, their own ambitions, their own dreams and fears. They should be allowed to choose their own futures.

GILES HIMSELF HAD visited the tribal area only once, during his earliest years as a journalist, when he heard rumors of a Jarawa woman having been raped near Tirur and felt compelled to investigate. He drove up to the village and asked the locals where he might encounter the Jarawa. They pointed him to a place just past the end of the road, a rice paddy with a stream at the far side and thick forest beyond. I realized that he was describing the same place where I had seen the visiting tribesmen, almost twenty years earlier.

Unlike me, however, Giles had decided to go farther in. He waded through the rice paddy to the stream, which was in full flood, bridged only by a single slippery tree trunk. Gingerly, he lay down prone and began to inch across it. Midway over, he was suddenly gripped with terror—of the stream, of the forest, and of the Jarawa themselves. He remembered the stories he had heard growing up, of murderous savages with poisoned arrows, and found himself immobilized, clenching the narrow log with his hands and knees. And now it was starting to rain.

Suddenly, a black shape leaped over his body—then another, then another. They were three Jarawa children, swift as deer, whose toes seemed barely to touch the wood before they hurtled up the forested hillside ahead, sprang over roots and fallen trees, and disappeared. Giles inched the rest of the way over, swung his legs down, and began stumbling uphill. The rain was coming down in torrents now. It took an hour to climb the slope that the children had run up in a minute or two. Finally, at the crest, he saw a large hut almost hidden in the trees, with smoke coming through the roof. Soaked and shaking with cold, he went inside to take shelter without pausing to think about what he was doing.

"There were the children I'd seen," he told me. "Three girls, and a woman resting beside them on the floor. I could see that her belly was swollen and made a sign to ask her if she were with child. She made a sign to say yes. Then she just lay there and looked at me, not moving. I was so cold and tired and scared that I was shivering. And I felt like I needed a smoke more than anything in the world."

Giles dug deep into his knapsack for a sodden matchbook and cigarette. He tried again and again to strike the match, but it would not light. "The woman was still watching me," he said. "Without saying a word, she picked up a stick from the fire and held it up until the burning part touched my cigarette. Now suddenly I was no longer afraid." One of the children smiled, and somehow, a few minutes later, he found himself playing with them. He stayed more than an hour. They clustered around to paint his face with ochre. The rain finally stopped, he left the hut and made his way back down the hillside, back toward the known world. He never learned the truth about the rape.

I asked him how the encounter had made him feel.

"It was one of the great experiences of my life," he said softly. He had never gone back.

That was when I decided to tell him about my long-ago journey to North Sentinel Island. After I finished the story, he asked many questions: Did they show hostility, or friendliness? Could I tell anything about their culture? Was it true that they are much taller than the Jarawa, as people say?

He asked one last question. This time, it was one I could answer: "What did it feel like to see them?"

"It was one of the greatest experiences of my life," I replied.

DESPITE THE GOVERNMENT'S recent strict policies to protect the Jarawa, I had heard that there was still a way that outsiders could sometimes see them. Before leaving Denis Giles's *Andaman Chronicle* office, I asked him whether he thought I should go.

"You saw them twenty years ago, so maybe you do need to see them now," the newspaperman said. "Maybe your intention of travel matters."

The problem was that I wasn't wholly certain what that was.

JOHN CHAU WAS a reader and a dreamer. Some of his favorite childhood books were mine as well, books about islands: Daniel Defoe's *Robinson Crusoe*, C. S. Lewis's *The Voyage of the Dawn Treader*. I remember wanting to be one of the young voyagers in that book, my favorite in the Narnia series, sailing farther than any ship had ever traveled, beyond the last island. They "saw the whole western sky lit up with an immense crimson sunset," Lewis wrote, "and thought of unknown lands on the Eastern rim of the world."

Chau's and my dreams were perhaps more similar than I would like to admit. I wondered whether even our trips to North Sentinel were also, in some unsettling way, similar. My journey was about the journey—about my own experience, not really about the Sentinelese themselves. There was nothing I could have learned about them on my clandestine voyage to the nearby waters, my glimpses of distant figures on the shore, that I could not have picked up simply by watching the old footage of T. N. Pandit and his companions meeting the islanders in the surf. I knew how my journey would end; I was following a script that was already written. Were Chau and I like the poachers who prowl the Andaman archipelago—poachers not of rare shells, but of experiences, glimmers of the sublime? We both went to the island to *look*, not to see.

Chau's blog, chronicling his many travels before the Andaman mission, is far more banal than sublime. He is "stoked"; his trips are "gnarly" and "dope." He seems far less a wandering prophet than just another California hiker bro. The handwritten diary of his final days, by contrast, reads like the testament of a half-crazed medieval saint: "God, I thank you for choosing me, before I was even yet formed in my mother's womb, to be Your messenger of Your Good News. . . . May Your Kingdom, Your Rule and Reign come now to North Sentinel Island."

Was my solo journey, too, a self-referential mission, shorn even of Chau's delusions of a divine calling? Unlike him, I had not gone to North Sentinel with the will to intrude. I had no blind impulse toward martyrdom—much less toward causing the harm that Chau might have selfishly inflicted by introducing disease among the islanders. My quest was not to shift the course of history, just to witness it.

The eighteen scrawled pages of Chau's Andaman journal—oddly reminiscent of Portman's diary—contain just one passage that resonates with my own experience of traveling to North Sentinel. It dates from the evening before his death, as he huddles in the fishing boat, wondering if the sunset he has just witnessed will be his last. He describes a waking vision that he had seen the night before: the image of a dark, island-like city bristling with jagged towers and teeming with human shapes. Then, with the sudden flash of a falling star, the city is illuminated, its darkness dissolving into celestial light. My journey, too, feels now—a quarter century later—like a momentary apparition, a collision of worlds.

To seek such a moment of sublime experience, when terror melts into awe and vast distances are bridged in an instant, may be a foundational human desire. A pardonable sin. The throb of an explorer's heart as he beholds an unknown coastline can set in pulsing motion a much greater sin, irrevocable, a quest for gold or glory with awful consequences. Think of Cortés or Columbus. But such an experience of wonder, some philosophers have argued, is also the prime mover of our species' quest for knowledge—and perhaps even our yearning, fitful as it may be, for human communion.

ONCE EACH DAY, a convoy of vehicles travels up the Andaman Trunk Road. Many of them carry tourists whose declared intention is to visit an official attraction called the Baratang Limestone Cave. Few of these people actually travel in order to see the Baratang Limestone Cave, which is as uninteresting as it is inaccessible.

And it certainly is inaccessible, at least by the usual standards of impatient day-trippers. Getting there requires leaving Port Blair two or three hours before dawn, rattling down miles of unpaved roads, and then queueing up with dozens of other cars, trucks, and buses at a police checkpoint, where officers require multiple copies of your photo ID, multiple signatures on documents pledging your adherence to the rules of travel through the tribal area, and a very detailed questionnaire to confirm your identity. *(Name. Date of birth. Place of birth. Name of father.)* The process takes about two hours, as people mill about drinking lukewarm tea and urinating into the road-side ditch. The huge automotive snake finally stirs and there is another hour of driving, an interminable wait for a ferry, a slow crossing, a long walk through steaming mangrove forest, and then thirty minutes in a narrow fissure, breathing the damp exhalations of a hundred other tourists, before you must turn around and repeat the entire process in reverse.

So certainly no one does this for the sake of the cave. Rather, they—we—do it for the hour or so midroute when our caravan passes through the Jarawa Tribal Reserve.

I hired an SUV and a driver—a wiry, taciturn man named Naga—to make the day trip. And the experience did quickly start to remind me, quite unsettlingly, of a safari that I took in Africa years ago. The same instructions: no throwing food, keep your doors locked, keep your windows up, keep your vehicle moving. The same intense scanning of my surroundings with inexpert eyes, as the guide points out what he knows I've come here to see.

It didn't take long before our first glimpse. Just seconds, really, after our vehicle entered the tribal reserve. Naga pointed: "Jarawa trail." A pathway wound up the hillside to our left, and at the top sat a big thatched hut, just like the ones I remembered seeing in Portman's photographs. Nearer to the road, a few small figures sat observing us, incuriously, like kids with nothing better to watch on TV. We drove on before I could see much more. The convoy moved at a good clip, too swift for my liking, with steep hillsides to our left and plunging gorges to our right.

Our second glimpse: somehow, another vehicle passed us in

the opposite direction on the narrow road. It was a Tribal Welfare truck, and the open back was full of Jarawa boys in shorts and T-shirts, all singing—a Hindi song, Naga told me. They were headed to one of the government schools.

It has been many years since any indigenous hunter took a shot at an *Inen*. These days, an anthropologist later told me, some Jarawa elders like to regale their grandchildren with songs and pantomimes narrating those bygone exploits, the olden times when brave bowmen raided frontier settlements by the light of the full moon. Deep in the forest, gathered together around of evening campfires, the tribe now weaves its own tales of discovery and contact.

We emerged from the jungle as quickly as we had entered it. I was carsick by now, and realizing that all I really wanted was to be back in Port Blair. As we awaited the ferry, people chattered excitedly about what we'd just seen. A nice-looking sixtyish couple from Mumbai came over. The wife: "My son was very upset with us when we told him we were going to do this. 'A human zoo.' But they are people, not animals. And we weren't going to visit the Andamans without seeing them."

I avoided a pair of Californian retirees among the bus passengers, one of whom was—quite literally—wearing a plastic pith helmet.

By the time we headed back on the Trunk Road, I was exhausted, hot, dehydrated. Our vehicle had no climate control, so I violated the rules and lowered a window to catch some of the cooler forest air. Just as I drifted into sleep, I was startled awake by a quick slowing of the SUV and an exclamation from Naga.

Right alongside the road, perhaps ten yards ahead of us, was a man. His skin was intensely black, and he was perhaps thirty-five or forty years old—old enough to have known a time before bus rides and bicultural schools—with a white-and-orange cloth tied loosely around his narrow waist. One of his hands held a long, curved bow, and over the opposite shoulder hung a quiver of arrows.

The first thing that registered with me was his body. Naked, perfect, as taut and upright as the bow. This is what a human body is supposed to be, I thought afterward. This is what our ancestors evolved toward for two million years. A body made to leap and climb, to chase and elude.

Then we passed, and the man was right alongside. My window was still rolled down, and it felt suddenly intimate to have our faces so close, no barrier between us. I did what seemed like the right thing in that moment—the polite, shared, human reflex—and smiled.

The hunter looked right through me, his eyes as cold as any I have ever seen.

MY PREVIOUS VISIT to the Andamans had felt like a journey. This one began to feel more and more like a trip. Are journeys even possible anymore, I wondered? Is it just that my heart has grown older and less expansive since the last century ended, or has the whole world?

While in Port Blair, I spent an entire day looking for Bala and his family. After the 2004 tsunami, I had feared the worst, remembering their frail hut a few hundred yards from the beach. But there was no way for me to contact them: I had lost the slip of paper with Bala's last name and address. All I remembered was the general area where their village had been, and the nearby cove with the fishing boats that had brought me to

North Sentinel. I also had a copy in my phone of a photo I had taken of Bala in 1998. With the help of an interpreter, I spent hours crisscrossing that part of Great Andaman, looking for anyone who might know of the family's fate. We could find no trace of the village; commercial sprawl from Port Blair seemed to have engulfed the area, and the interpreter told me that no one lived in thatched huts or fished in boats like that anymore. Many of the people we spoke with were surprised to hear that I had visited the Andamans so long ago, and wanted to know what it was like in those days—most of the islands' inhabitants seemed either to be too young to remember the twentieth century, or to have arrived from the mainland after the tsunami.

At last, someone directed us to a quayside where half a dozen grizzled old men squatted in a low shed, mending their fishing nets. They took turns peering at the picture on my phone. Finally, one of the men looked up and told my interpreter that he remembered Bala, his wife, and their three sons. They had been unharmed in the tsunami, he said, but Bala had lost his fishing boat and his livelihood. Like many islanders after the 2004 cataclysm, the family had departed to join relatives on the mainland. It was unlikely there was anyone left who would know their current whereabouts. They had melted away into the ocean of a billion citizens of India.

THERE WAS STILL another place I wanted to visit before leaving, one that hadn't been accessible to me in 1998. Little Andaman Island lies at the far southern end of the archipelago, a lonely scrap of land. I'd been told in Port Blair that it was a place where I could find the old Andamans, the frontier Andamans of twenty or fifty years ago. Getting there requires an overnight eighty-mile journey on a sporadic ferryboat. It had remained closed to foreigners until just two years before, when the Modi government, in a move to boost tourism, lifted restrictions on almost thirty islands in the archipelago.

I already knew Little Andaman from Maurice Vidal Portman's diaries. It was the remotest place he had explored—a place where, he claimed, he had singlehandedly "tamed" the native Onge. I imagined him there walking the pristine sand, playing Schubert on his violin.

I didn't plan to visit the descendants of the indigenes Portman had met, however. They live now in a restricted tribal reserve at the southern end of the island; these onetime hunter-gatherers now depend largely on food supplied by the Indian authorities. Malnutrition rates, alcoholism, and infant mortality are reportedly high. In 2008, at least eight Onge men and boys—almost a tenth of the tribe's remaining population—died after drinking the contents of a bottle that they had found on the beach, which they believed to be an alcoholic beverage; it was actually a toxic chemical solvent.

I'd heard that Little Andaman was the place where John Chau stayed during the weeks before his doomed mission. He believed it was the best place in the islands to keep a low profile. He also thought it was the best place to train his mind and body: the one most similar to North Sentinel of any he could reach.

As the ferry approached the quay at dawn and passengers disembarked at the little settlement of Hut Bay, I found a place that felt, at first, like the old Andamans I remembered. Towering trees hemmed the gleaming beach. The island had almost no cars; locals navigated the potholed roads on mopeds or hitched rides in rattletrap jeeps. A big construction project was

Connecting the undersea fiber optic cable at Hut Bay,
Little Andaman Island, January 2020.

Indian fishermen on the Andaman Sea, Little Andaman Island, January 2020.

underway in the harbor—a new jetty?—but the ramshackle shops in the bazaar, with their quaint signs ("K.R. NATHAN & CO., GENERAL MERCHANTS") gave the satisfying impression of a movie set from an old Western. I found a family-owned guesthouse, really just a row of tin-roofed cubicles, each with a sagging cot, a plastic chair, and a mosquito net. It felt like exactly what I needed. At last, too, I seemed to have found a place with no cell service whatsoever. I tossed my iPhone into the bottom of my rucksack and felt a rush of joy to think of it lying there for the next week or so: an inert, irrelevant black brick.

A line of towering trees stood across the road from the guesthouse, with glimpses of the beach beyond. I set out to explore and soon felt like I was in Portman's world. The tallest of the trees, no doubt, were here when he landed. The buttress roots of the largest behemoth reminded me of those in his photographs of North Sentinel, the ones with ersatz Sentinelese hunters crouching against the monstrous pale roots.

As I drew closer to the ocean, though, I found that this place was far from primeval. Heaps of trash drifted like snow in the niches and crannies of the buttress roots: lost flip-flops, tampon applicators, and—most of all—dozens upon dozens of discarded water bottles. The beach itself was even worse: I almost stepped on the daggerlike shard of an industrial-size lightbulb. Several days later, one of the locals told me that the flotsam mostly came from far away, drifting on the prevailing currents. An inspection of the water bottles on the sand proved he was right. A few had floated over from the Indian mainland, more from Thailand, Burma, Bangladesh, Malaysia. The plastic castoffs on a hundred yards of this beach probably represented more human beings than have lived on North Sentinel Island for the past thousand years. Surely the same trash washes onto the beach there. The Jarawa language, even before the tribe was in regular contact with the outside world, had developed its own term for Styrofoam: *the white wood of the sea.*

Still, I found some peace on Little Andaman. My phone stayed in my bag. The sun rose early there—before 4:00 a.m.—but I was up most mornings to watch it break the horizon of the Indian Ocean, go swimming, and then sit on the plastic chair outside my cabin and write in my journal. The family that ran the guesthouse was friendly and kind, and I was their only guest. The husband, Jogesh, told me in broken English about his early years on Little Andaman, in the 1970s, when a few thousand Hindu refugees from East Bengal were settled here to clear the land for coconut plantations. His wife spoke no English at all and stayed in the kitchen, cooking delicious fish curries and fried plantains. Their two sons, Santu and Atanu, were in their mid-twenties; they came and went on their mopeds. Every evening, Jogesh blew a conch shell that summoned the family to prayer.

One night after dinner, Atanu, the older brother, lingered to chat. He asked me questions about myself and told me proudly that although he'd lived most of his life on Little Andaman— and had only been to the Indian mainland once—he'd earned a degree from a small technical college on Great Andaman. Now he was a construction site supervisor, working on the big underwater cable project.

This, it turned out, was the construction I had noticed down in the harbor at Hut Bay: the terminus of a high-speed fiber line that would run fifteen hundred miles from the mainland, bringing 4G service to the archipelago. By the end of the month, it would reach Great Andaman, at a terminal in Corbyn's Cove, one of the dwindling number of places in the islands still named after some long-dead Englishman: the assiduous keeper of the Andaman Home.*

The connection at Little Andaman would take a bit longer—maybe several months. Atanu couldn't wait.

"You know, I'm twenty-seven years old and I don't know how to use the internet," he said, indignation rising in his voice. He felt marooned here on his native island. He had heard about Facebook and YouTube but never used them. Now, at last, he would join the modern world.

I FORMED A stronger bond with Atanu's brother, Santu—two years younger and smaller, quieter, with an adolescent wisp of mustache. He hadn't gone to college; his only work now was as a part-time mail carrier. And unlike Atanu, who talked mostly about the future, Santu dwelled mainly on the past.

One evening, I mentioned that I wanted to get away from the beach a bit and explore the inland of Little Andaman. The next morning, he offered to take me. We rode a mile or so on his moped to the trailhead, at a place where the palm-oil plantations met the forest. We weren't really supposed to venture farther, he said—too many people had gotten lost back here—but he knew the way well.

Before long, the second-growth trees gave way to deep jungle. As we walked, Santu pointed out different species,

---

* The nineteenth-century British colonizers loved to stake claims on immortality by naming geographical features after themselves: there is still a Portman Bay on Rutland Island, south of Port Blair. Colonel R.C. Tytler, an avid ornithologist, delighted himself with bestowing his name on various species and subspecies, including a leaf warbler (*Phylloscopus tytleri*) and a barn swallow (*Hirundo rustica tytleri*), as well as a small lizard and two different types of frogs.

telling me their names in both Hindi and English: the clustered orchids, the slow, furry bees, and the lizards so unused
to humans that they didn't run away when we reached out to
touch them, until the moment that our fingers grazed their
backs. He told me which plants could be woven to make the
wall of a house, which ones his mother made into pickles, which
ones you should rub on a cut to make it heal, and which one his
schoolteachers had used on him when he misbehaved.

These are things that all the kids of his generation on Little
Andaman learned, he said. They were the things your parents
taught you so you could start making your way capably through
the world. Santu spoke of his childhood as if he were an old
man recalling a faraway time.

He told me about the day that everything changed on the
island. Santu was ten years old then, and Atanu twelve. They
were playing near their house when they heard their aunt
shouting from next door. A big wave was coming, and they
needed to run. The brothers could see it in the distance, and
they sprinted as fast as they could away from the beach, toward
higher ground. Three or four minutes later, the tsunami came.
It engulfed every house near the shoreline—everything that
Santu's family owned was lost forever. Fallen logs and fishing
boats became hurtling projectiles that ran people down as they
fled.

They had rebuilt—and were proud of how much of their old
lives they were able to reconstruct—but things were never quite
the same. There seemed to be fewer fish in the ocean now, and
more trash. Kids no longer explored in the forest; the island
had better infrastructure, and families could get televisions.
Some bought cell phones, too. I was surprised—I'd thought
there was no coverage at all on Little Andaman. That wasn't

quite true, Santu said. If you knew just the right spots along the beach, you could find a signal. Kids got phones so that they could watch movies. It might take all weekend to download, but once you had a couple of good ones, you could join the popular clique who clustered together, watching.

Santu didn't like how things had changed, admitting that even he spent more time indoors now, and much less time out exploring. He was embarrassed to admit that more than a year had passed since he'd hiked this trail.

"You know when the last time was?" he asked me. "You know about the American guy, Chau?"

I told him I did.

"John Allen Chau," he said, as if proud that he knew the whole name. "I took him out here. You know he stayed at our guesthouse?"

I didn't. So he had spent his time on Little Andaman with this family—with these four people who were starting to feel like my family.

Chau lingered a week or so here before going back to Port Blair to meet the fishermen who helped him make his final journey. Except for that one hike, Santu said, the American kept to himself. He took breakfast with the family, then went out to run on the beach, to swim, and to ride around the island on his motorbike. Maybe he went to the Christian church in Hut Bay. He never mentioned the Sentinelese. Never brought up religion.

I asked what he and Chau talked about on their hike. "He was interested in mysterious places," Santu said. "I told him that I was, too. That I wanted to travel to the pyramids in Egypt, and the city on a mountain in Brazil. But just mysterious places. Not unknown."

We both fell silent. We had stopped at a wide spot in the trail. The fact of Chau's death—of that other American's death—hung heavy in the air between us.

The police came afterward, he said. They spent a couple of days interrogating the family about the strange young foreigner.

I asked Santu whether any of them cried when they heard the news. He didn't answer.

I asked whether his family said prayers for John Chau.

He made a soft sound that I thought was a yes.

SANTU WAS OFTEN up at daybreak. He went down to the beach with his dog, Rani. They chased each other around and played in the surf, and I would see them sometimes when I came down early to swim.

One morning, a few days after our jungle hike, I walked to the beach and found Santu and Rani there, as usual. But this time, the young man and his dog weren't playing in the surf. They were sitting together companionably on a high, broad promontory of rocks, beneath a bulletwood tree. Santu had his knees drawn up, his head down.

I walked over and asked him what he was doing. Santu looked up, embarrassed. He had been hunched over his phone, hoping for a signal.

IN THE FIRST days after Chau's death, many evangelical groups denied any association with his ill-fated journey. He was not even an authentic missionary, they said—merely a lone eccentric. Newspaper reports, too, made him sound less like an apostle of the Gospel than just another hyped-up, dim-witted

American backpacker, the kind who would fall off a cliff trying to take a selfie.

But in the weeks and months that followed, some evangelicals began to publicly embrace Chau. In April 2019, a Kansas City–based organization called All Nations, whose stated vision is "to see Jesus worshipped by all the peoples of the earth," held a fundraiser in his memory; one of the organization's staff members performed a song in which he imagined Chau and the Sentinelese worshiping together around Christ's heavenly throne.

In fact, as journalists dug deeper into the story of his death, they learned that far from acting alone, Chau had received guidance and support dating back to his undergraduate days working with the Missions and Outreach department at Oral Roberts University. He undertook extensive training at an All Nations boot camp, where inductees were taught to strive for a "wartime mentality" befitting crusaders going forth into battle against the forces of Satan. One role-playing exercise involved confronting a village of "natives" armed with fake spears. Chau also received language training at another missionary-run school—perhaps where he learned the few words of Xhosa that would fail to gain him much traction with the Sentinelese.

Some of Chau's missionary friends said that he had been obsessed with the idea of bringing the Gospel to the islanders since he was a teenager, and even imagined himself residing permanently on North Sentinel. He traveled to the Andamans on reconnaissance several times, and before his final trip, he drafted a twenty-seven-step plan for Christianizing the Sentinelese, which he shared with a small circle of supporters.

Even after Chau's untimely demise, some evangelicals continued to urge further missions to North Sentinel. Paying tribute to Chau on the first anniversary of his death, the head of a missionary program at Baptist Bible College in Missouri wrote: "My prayer for and plea to my students is that they would catch the spirit of John Chau." Moreover, he called upon other evangelicals to take up the young martyr's "holy task," benefiting from the experiences chronicled in his diary: "Let's think fairly about Chau's preparation and strategy, then improve upon those things, if possible."

A year later, a member of a group called The Gospel Coalition admitted that Chau had not only broken Indian law in pursuit of his evangelical mission, but also risked transmitting some deadly disease to those he sought to convert. Still, the writer argued, this is a perfectly acceptable risk: the fate of the islanders' immortal souls weighs more than their mere earthly survival.

Surely anyone with a modicum of sanity and human decency recoils from this. But I should confess that in my more pessimistic moments, I have sometimes wondered whether Chau's secular critics—all the well-meaning bloggers, tweeters, and activists who want the outside world to leave North Sentinel Island in eternal isolation—are just as delusional, just as much in thrall to their own mythology. Visions of the Sentinelese dwelling in happy perpetuity on their island are probably almost as unrealistic as visions of them dancing eternally with John Chau around the throne of Jesus.

For the truth is that we—the other eight billion human inhabitants of this planet—are already encroaching inexorably on their tiny preserve, as relentlessly and recklessly as in the days of Maurice Portman. Climate scientists predict that rising sea levels may leave much of the Andaman archipelago underwater within less than a century. Global warming, overfishing, pollution, and plastic debris will continue a campaign of devastation against the plants and animals that North Sentinel's inhabitants depend on to survive. The island's perfect isolation, unmoored from ordinary space and time, is our own self-consoling fantasy: as long as the Sentinelese remain, we can tell ourselves that our planet is still, to some tiny degree, inviolate. We see those islanders through vision as fogged with our own preoccupations as Columbus's first glimpses of the Caribs.

Yet within all the enveloping layers of myth and meme, a small stubborn truth remains: the inarguable fact of their persistence. Their presence in our world enlarges the boundaries of what it means to be human. Holding fast to a few square miles of their planet, they declare their independence. With eyes as shrewd as any explorer's, the Sentinelese look at all that we have to offer them—our planes, our plastics, our inflatable boats, and our waterproof Bibles—and say: *Thanks anyway. We'd rather not.*

I ENDED UP lingering on Little Andaman longer than I'd planned. Finally, I realized that I was going to miss my flights home if I didn't take the next ferry back to Port Blair. Now I had only one evening and half a morning on the big island before starting the trip to Kolkata, Delhi, Dubai, and Washington.

I realized that there was something I'd been postponing throughout my stay in the Andamans, avoiding it without even being conscious of the fact: catching another glimpse of North Sentinel Island, if only from afar.

There was no time to reach Wandoor—the beach where I'd met Bala twenty-two years earlier, where the island might be

Sunrise, Little Andaman Island, January 2020.

visible on a clear day. Then I thought of Mount Harriet, the steep hill above Port Blair where the Chief Commissioner's villa once stood: the place where a dying captive once sat, looking toward North Sentinel, pining wordlessly for home.

According to a tourist map, Mount Harriet's summit was a scenic overlook now. Very early on the morning of my departure, I hired a driver to take me. We wound our way up the hillside, reached a trailhead, and set out on foot.

No trace remained of the Commissioner's villa. Not of the view, either. A stubby watchtower, half hidden among the trees, afforded nothing but a slightly higher vantage of the surrounding forest. There was little to see here—but much to hear: The fretful conversations of birds. The voices of insects, rising as the sun rose, too. Palm leaves stirring in the freshening breeze. The incongruous music from someone's boom box, far away downhill.

I closed my eyes and listened for a while, until the impatient driver, who'd been following five steps behind and seemed increasingly agitated by my silent reverie, coaxed me back to where we'd parked the car. As we made our way down the mountain, I was flooded with a sense of relief—mingled, just moments later, with regret.

Not long afterward, while waiting at the airport for my Kolkata flight, it occurred to me that I might have one more chance to catch a parting glimpse. Planes bound from Port Blair to the mainland sometimes swing southward a bit as they climb toward cruising altitude. Often this takes them right past North Sentinel, and on a clear day, passengers can get a good look. Anyone on the island would get a good look at the aircraft, too.

Our plane was nearly full. Perhaps a hundred and fifty of

us would be fellow travelers: one of the countless temporary tribes that recombine daily in every airport on earth, strangers joining fortunes for an hour or two. My cabinmates were nearly all vacationers, returning sunburnt and satiated from the archipelago to their homes on the Indian mainland. A young couple across the aisle—obviously newlyweds—leaned close together, still just a little bashful, taking selfies. Buckled in, I tapped my foot anxiously. Would this be one of those flights?

At last, our plane taxied, straightened, sped, and made its small miraculous leap into the morning sky. When we began a wide swing toward the south and west, rising above Port Blair's smoggy haze into the clear tropical air, it became obvious that this *was* going to be one of those flights. We were about to see North Sentinel, and it was about to see us.

But suddenly, I realized that my seat was on the wrong side of the plane: starboard, not port. As we dipped into our turn, people across the aisle were peering out the windows, pointing, and taking their phones out to snap pictures. The young husband whispered excitedly to his bride. Strapped into my seat just a few feet away, I could only watch them watching.

The plane's wings straightened, we rose, and the island slipped away, unseen. Another journey had begun: into the terra incognita of the sky, toward my own distant home.

"Jack Andaman," from the title page of Frederic J. Mouat's
Adventures and Researches Among the Andaman Islanders,
*1863. Image based on an 1858 photograph by Oscar Mallitte,
Calcutta, now in the Royal Collection at Windsor Castle.*

SOURCES AND ADDENDA

Despite the outsize niche that North Sentinel Island fills in millions of people's imaginations, this is the first full-length book on it that has ever been published.

The travel writer's instinct is always to *go there*. He sets his boots on the ground of a place, experiences it with his own senses, encounters its inhabitants on their own turf and their own terms. With North Sentinel Island, that wasn't quite possible. At times, I have felt more like an astronomer, straining for signals from a familiar-yet-distant planet; even my close encounter with the island's sandy shore was an orbit rather than a landing. Still, while I regret not being able to trace much of the island's interior landscape—let alone the inner lives and thoughts of the islanders—I have worked hard, over the course of many years, to chart its surrounding geography, both literal and otherwise.

While traveling in the Andaman Islands and mainland India in 1998 and 2020, I filled many notebooks with details that I have drawn on for this book. My usual practice was to jot down rough notes on the spot—for instance, when conducting an interview—and then write up more polished journal entries within the next day or two. All my renderings of conversations are drawn directly from those notes, including when I quote speakers of non-standard English. (There is just one major exception: my 1998 conversations with T. N. Pandit were all transcribed directly from audio recordings.) I have also, of course, benefited from the hundreds of photographs that I took on both trips.

Some parts of *The Last Island* appeared originally in a long article that I published in *The American Scholar* in 2000. Any reader who closely compares the two might notice some small factual discrepancies; in nearly all cases they are because I have corrected minor errors. The one exception is that in the article I used a pseudonym to protect Bala's identity. After a quarter century, and with Bala and his family no longer living in the Andamans, it seems safe to restore his actual given name.

My *American Scholar* article was published under the title "The Last Island of the Savages." I intended for the offensive term "savages" to be understood as an ironic commentary on the tendency of outsiders, especially Westerners, to both fear and fetishize the inhabitants of places like North Sentinel. (I also hoped that readers would catch my implication that the behavior of foreign interlopers, especially the British, was often far more "savage" than that of the indigenous Andamanese.) For various reasons—not least, to avoid possible misinterpretation—I have given my book a different title.

This book covers the complicated history and geography of an island chain that many non-Indians have barely heard of, if at all. With that in mind, I have taken the liberty of streamlining a few details so as not to confuse such readers. Most significant, I think, is that while I refer in several places to the Andaman Islands as an offshore territory of India, the full official name of the territory is the Andaman and Nicobar Islands, since it includes a smaller island group, about a hundred miles south of Great Andaman. (The Nicobars have a distinct history and are home to indigenous groups that have no close genetic or cultural affinities with the native Andamanese.) Another geographical simplification: While I refer to Great Andaman a couple of times as an island, many sources describe it as an archipelago within the broader Andaman archipelago, encompassing not just the central cluster of North, Middle, and South Andaman (divided from one another by narrow tidal creeks), but also several smaller nearby islands (not including North Sentinel). I have also left out an episode of the Andamans' colonial history, which is that in the late eighteenth century, the British briefly attempted to establish an outpost near what is now Port Blair, an effort that they abandoned after a few years, in 1796, due to disease and lack of supplies. There is no record of any direct interaction with the Sentinelese during that period.

In referring to various indigenous Andamanese communities, I have used the tribal names common among outsiders (including contemporary anthropologists), which were first bestowed by nineteenth-century Englishmen. Some of those designations—such as *Sentinelese*, obviously—are entirely foreign inventions. As noted in Chapter Three, *Jarawa* derives from a misunderstanding: it means "the other people" in the dialect of a nearby Great Andamanese tribe that was friendlier to the British. The Jarawa simply use the term *Aung*—which means "the people"—in referring collectively to themselves. Likewise, the name *Onge*, commonly used by outsiders for the tribe inhabiting Little Andaman, means "the people" in that island's indigenous language. Members of the community typically distinguish themselves from others with the term *Eniregale*, which means "perfect person."

General Sources

Thirty years ago, as a college senior, I was fortunate to take a course on the Age of Discovery taught by Stephen Greenblatt at Harvard. His analysis of that history—especially in his pathbreaking book *Marvelous Possessions: The Wonder of the New World* (University of Chicago Press, 1991; revised edition 2017)—has had a deep and enduring impact on my own understanding of European exploration and exploitation in foreign climes, especially the experience of "first contact." It was also in Greenblatt's class that I first read the texts that cast their long shadow across so many other narratives: Christopher Columbus's accounts of his four voyages to the New World. I have returned to them many times over the years, while also benefiting from Laurence Bergreen's *Columbus: The Four Voyages* (New York: Viking, 2011) and Samuel Eliot Morison's landmark *Admiral of the Ocean Sea: A Life of Christopher Columbus* (Boston: Little, Brown, 1942).

In the earliest years of my research on Andamanese history and anthropology, I benefited greatly from the work and personal assistance of the late George H. J. Weber, a Swiss businessman and enthusiastic independent scholar. In the 1990s, Weber founded an organization called the Andaman Association to foster research on the islands. As far as I could tell, the group only ever had one consistent active member—Weber himself—but with extraordinary assiduity, he mined museums, libraries, and scholarly journals for all the sources he could find about the archipelago's indigenous tribes. He presented this research on a sprawling website called Lonely Islands (www.andaman.org). Sadly, the Andaman Association and its website went defunct around 2009, several years before Weber's death, but most of the Lonely Islands webpages remain accessible online via the Wayback Machine. Weber's work is an especially rich resource on early explorers of the archipelago and their encounters with the natives. His carefully prepared inventories of Andaman-related manuscripts and artifacts scattered around the world are unrivaled by any other source, whether printed or digital.

Anyone who sets out to explore the challenging terrain of Andamanese history will soon find himself scaling the steep slopes of Maurice Vidal Portman's two-volume, nine-hundred-page *A History of Our Relations with the Andamanese: Compiled from Histories and Travels, and from the Records of the Government of India* (Calcutta: Office of the Superintendent of Government Printing, 1899). The eccentric explorer, linguist, colonial official, and self-taught anthropologist compiled what often seems like every Western account of interactions with the native tribes, from the era of Claudius Ptolemy through the nineteenth century. His book can be frustrating to use, as it lacks both an index and, in many sections, any discernible logical or chronological structure. Its terminology is frequently confusing, since Portman sometimes uses "Jarawa" to refer to various uncontacted groups in the outer islands of the archipelago, including Little Andaman and North Sentinel. Yet it remains invaluable, and while working on this book, I spent many hours combing through its pages, including for my accounts of contacts with the Andamanese through the centuries and decades preceding Portman's own arrival. (See my notes on Chapter Five for more Portman-related sources.)

Portman was not, fortunately, the only outside anthropologist ever to study the Andamanese. Of particular note is A. R. Radcliffe-Brown's *The Andaman Islanders: A Study in Social*

Anthropology (Cambridge University Press, 1922), which is considered a twentieth-century landmark in the discipline— less so for his specific insights about the tribal people than for his methodology, which aimed (with mixed success) to present findings based on systematic fieldwork and intensive, holistic observation rather than impressions and anecdotes. In the 1960s, Lidio Cipriani's *The Andaman Islanders* (New York: Praeger, 1966) described the prevalence of homosexual activity among the natives, as well as other previously undocumented elements of their culture.

Among all the anthropologists who have conducted research in the Andaman Islands, however, the most exceptional surely must be Vishvajit Pandya, who has spent considerable time among the indigenous tribes—first the Onge, more recently the Jarawa—over the past four decades, learning their languages and participating in their cultural traditions. Of all the books and articles that I have read about the Andamans, his are the only ones that make me feel that I am starting to get a sense of what it is like to *be* Andamanese: to see the outside world through native eyes rather than just peering at the natives through the eyes of an outsider. Two of Pandya's books were particularly rich sources for my own: *Above the Forest: A Study of Andamanese Ethnoanemology, Cosmology, and the Power of Ritual* (Oxford University Press, 1993) and *In the Forest: Visual and Material Worlds of Andamanese History (1858–2006)* (University Press of America, 2009). Although circumstances prevented us from meeting in person while I was in India, I am grateful to him for sharing his richly nuanced insights by email and phone.

Madhusree Mukerjee's *The Land of Naked People: Encounters with Stone Age Islanders* (Boston: Houghton Mifflin, 2003) offers an accessible, vigorously reported overview of the Andamanese tribes at the turn of the millennium. (It bears pointing out, however, that the Andamanese are really not "stone age" in any sense.) A journalist with *Scientific American*, Mukerjee made several visits to the archipelago, including a clandestine circumnavigation of North Sentinel Island that was, in her telling, uncannily similar to the one I had made several years earlier.

Chapter 1

In the chapter's first epigraph, I have used my own translation of a short Greek passage from Plutarch's *Life of Sertorius* (9:1).

For my account of the MV *Primrose*'s misadventure, I am grateful to Captain Robert Fore, who piloted the rescue helicopter. I also drew on other interviews (including with Regent Shipping Company staff) and contemporary newspaper reports. The Library of Congress's Geography and Map Division was a rich source of early maps of the Indian Ocean, as were the British Library and several rare-book dealers in Britain and the United States.

In addition to Stephen Greenblatt's *Marvelous Possessions*, other texts that provide valuable insight on first contacts, from the perspectives of both indigenous people and outsiders, include Marshall Sahlins's *Islands of History* (University of Chicago Press, 1986); Daniel K. Richter's *Facing East from Indian Country: A Native History of Early America* (Harvard University Press, 2001); John Sutton Lutz's *Myth and Memory: Stories of Indigenous-European Contact* (UBC Press, 2008); James Axtell's *Natives and Newcomers: The Cultural Origins of North America* (Oxford University Press, 2001); Neal Salisbury's

Manitou and Providence: Indians, Europeans, and the Making of New England, 1500–1643 (Oxford University Press, 1982); and Frederick W. Turner's *Beyond Geography: The Western Spirit Against the Wilderness* (New York: Viking, 1980). The powerful 1983 Australian documentary film *First Contact* chronicles such a moment in the highlands of New Guinea—including its tragic misunderstandings and fatal consequences—while the fictionalized Hollywood portrayal of an extraterrestrial landing in *Arrival* (2016) inspires reflection on how fantasies of first contact continue to exert their strong pull on the twenty-first-century imagination.

The eventful *National Geographic* expedition to the Andamans is recounted in that magazine's July 1975 issue, as well as depicted in the documentary *Man in Search of Man*, released that same year.

The lengthy quotation on page 21 ("It is impossible to imagine any human beings to be lower in the scale of civilization . . .") can be found in *The Andaman Islands, with Notes on Barren Island* (Calcutta: Baptist Mission Press, 1859).

For information on modern-day "uncontacted tribes," the work of the global nonprofits Survival International and Cultural Survival—which carefully monitor the status of indigenous peoples and advocate for their welfare—has been invaluable. Another helpful source is a 2013 report by another nonprofit, the International Work Group for Indigenous Affairs, "Indigenous People in Voluntary Isolation and Initial Contact," as well as a related document, "Indigenous People in Voluntary Isolation and Initial Contact in the Americas: Recommendations for the Full Respect of Their Human Rights," produced by the Organization of American States and the Inter-American Commission on Human Rights." The work of anthropologist Stuart Kirsch provides important insights into the cultural role of the "lost tribes" concept. (See especially "Lost Tribes: Indigenous People and the Social Imaginary," *Anthropological Quarterly*, April 1997.) A counter-argument to isolation policy is presented in Robert S. Walker et al., "Are Isolated Indigenous Peoples Headed Toward Extinction?" (*PLoS One*, 2016).

Andamanese genetics—which may ultimately solve the stubborn mystery of the indigenous tribes' origins—have received surprisingly little scholarly attention. That is largely because access to the islands, and to DNA samples collected by the Indian government, remains tightly restricted. I am grateful to Nick Patterson of the Harvard-MIT Broad Institute for speaking with me about his studies in progress (it was he who compared the Sentinelese to the Hapsburgs), as well as to David Reich of Harvard, whose work on the subject can be found in his article "Reconstructing Indian Population History" (co-authored with Patterson and others, *Nature*, September 2009) and his book *Who We Are and How We Got Here: Ancient DNA and the New Science of the Human Past* (New York: Pantheon, 2018). For an archaeological perspective on Andamanese prehistory and possible origins, see Zarine Cooper, *Archaeology and History: Early Settlements in the Andaman Islands* (Oxford University Press, 2002).

My accounts of John Chau's ill-fated mission, in both Chapters One and Six, draw mainly on his own handwritten travel journal, which his family released to the press shortly after his death. I also benefited from widely published newspaper accounts, especially those written by Jeffrey Gettleman, India bureau chief of the *New York Times*. Two helpful magazine features were published some months later in *Outside* (Alex Perry,

"The Last Days of John Allen Chau," July 2019) and *GQ* (Doug Bock Clark, "The American Missionary and the Uncontacted Tribe," August 2019).

Chapter 2

Triloknath "T. N." Pandit graciously spent many hours speaking with me in 1998 and in 2021–22, sharing memories of his journeys to North Sentinel Island and the Jarawa territory on Middle Andaman, as well as other chapters of his life and career. He chronicled some of his encounters with the islanders in his fifty-page book *The Sentinelese* (Calcutta: Anthropological Survey of India, 1990).

Others who offered recollections of those trips included the late Bakhtawar Singh of the Andaman Bush Police, as well as Anstice Justin of the Anthropological Survey of India. (As a "tribal" person from the nearby Nicobar Islands, Justin was able to lend particularly enlightening perspective.) Contemporary accounts of the missions can be found in the Indian press, including two local newspapers, the *Daily Telegrams* and *Light of Andamans*, back issues of which I consulted at the publications' respective offices in Port Blair. Rare footage of one contact mission appears in Aruna HarPrasad's 1995 documentary "The Tribes of the Andaman and Nicobar Islands."

For indigenous people's interpretations of Europeans' arrival, including at Manhattan Island, see James Axtell's *Beyond 1492: Encounters in Colonial North America* (Oxford University Press, 1992), as well as Julia Blackburn's *The White Men: The First Response of Aboriginal Peoples to the White Man* (New York: HarperCollins, 1979). See General Sources, above, for Vishvajit Pandya's brilliant work reconstructing how the Andamanese experienced early visits from outsiders. The description of Andamanese *lau* is from Radcliffe-Brown's *The Andaman Islanders*; Pandya corroborated this for me as well.

A fascinating book by the anthropologist Sita Venkateswar, *Development and Ethnocide: Colonial Practices in the Andaman Islands* (Copenhagen: International Work Group on Indigenous Affairs, 2004) includes her field notes from interviews in 1992 with Onge elders sharing memories and oral traditions of the Little Andaman tribe's history. One of them spoke of a white *Inen* named "Etonoye," a "big man" who had repeatedly visited the island in a boat, taking photographs and bringing knives, matches, and other useful things. On one occasion, the Onge informant said, an islander shot one of Etonoye's *Ineny* companions with an arrow, after which the white men returned to shoot "big iron balls" into the forest. Venkateswar speculates that Etonoye may have been M. V. Portman, and the altercation recounted by her informant resembles at least two clashes on Little Andaman described in Portman's private diary.

Chapter 3

The southern Jarawa's emergence from the forests of Great Andaman—some of which I witnessed firsthand in 1998—has since been chronicled in various publications, including K. Mukhopadhyay, R. K. Bhattacharya, and B. N. Sarkar, eds., *Jarawa Contact: Ours with Them, Theirs with Us* (Kolkata: Anthropological Survey of India, 2002); and Pronob Kumar Sircar, *Jarawa: The Struggle Continues* (New Delhi: Akansha Publishing, 2011). Ratan Chandra Kar, the medical officer whom I met at Kadamtala in 1998 and Port Blair in 2020, has published a valuable firsthand account of his experiences among the Kadamtala Jarawa, *The Jarawas of the Andamans* (third edition, Kolkata, 2018), including observations on the spread of disease during the period after contact. Madhusree Mukerjee's *The Land of Naked People* (see General Sources, above) presents a journalist's account drawn from her reporting in the early 2000s. The 2010 volume *Jarawa Tribal Reserve Dossier: Cultural & Biological Diversities in the Andaman Islands* (Paris: UNESCO), edited by Pankaj Sekhsaria and Vishvajit Pandya, offers a variety of perspectives on the tribe's past, present, and possible future.

In chapters 5 and 7 of *In the Forest* (see General Sources), Pandya provides a characteristically nuanced view of Enmei's story, in which he treats with some skepticism the notion that the Jarawa teenager was the prime mover of his tribe's change of heart toward outsiders. He also provides a somewhat different account of the boy's injury and removal to the Port Blair hospital. Pandya benefited from conversations with Enmei and other eyewitnesses (both Jarawa and Indian) in 1999 and the years following, and his book even includes two fascinating pencil drawings done by Enmei—one depicting the hospital, the other a scene in the tribal reserve. Ultimately, he admits, the true reason for the Jarawa's emergence "depends on who tells [the story] and when." (Note that there is no standardized spelling of Enmei's name: various written sources refer to him as Enmey, Enmay, En Mei, etc.)

Chapter 4

By their very nature, most imperial powers produce gigantic quantities of documentation, and nineteenth-century British India was no exception. Indeed, the sheer volume of its surviving paperwork is enough to inspire awe. There are official reports (daily, weekly, monthly, annual, decennial); orders and counterorders; complaints and remonstrances; financial tabulations (reckoned to the last copper *pie*, or 1/192 of a rupee); military dispatches; viceregal edicts; shipping manifests. The British Library contains the vast files of the former India Office—the London-based nerve center of the Raj—which fill ten miles or so of shelf space. The National Archives of India (NAI), established in the nineteenth century as the Imperial Record Department, holds an immense number of administrative documents left behind by the British. The record groups "Home Department—Port Blair Branch" and "Home Department—Judicial" proved especially rich troves of information on daily doings in the Andaman settlement from its earliest days. I was fortunate to spend time in both London and New Delhi delving into those two inexhaustible collections.

The Home Department records at the NAI provided a great deal of unpublished material on the Andaman Committee's 1857 expedition, the capture of "Jack Andaman," and the unfortunate native's short stay in Calcutta. In London, I caught further glimpses of Jack in the papers of Charlotte, Lady Canning, wife of the first viceroy, including both her private journal and her correspondence with Queen Victoria.

(That precious trove barely escaped incineration in December 1859, when the Cannings were on their way across northern India with a retinue of soldiers, servants, and elephants. One night by the roadside in Rajasthan, Lady Canning's tent caught fire. An accomplished artist and writer, the countess rushed back into the flames to rescue her sketchbooks and papers, including her cherished correspondence with Queen Victoria. The monarch's letters, penned on crested stationery from Windsor Castle and Buckingham Palace, are charred around the edges. One afternoon at the British Library, a reading room attendant handed me a thick folder full of them, with as little fanfare as if it had been a Tube ticket.)

Published sources on the 1857 expedition include Frederic J. Mouat's *Adventures and Researches Among the Andaman Islanders* (London: Hurst & Blackett, 1863), as well as *The Andaman Islands, with Notes on Barren Island* (Calcutta: Baptist Mission Press, 1859). In the early 2000s, a curator in the Royal Collection at Windsor Castle rediscovered the original photographs from the expedition—including three portraits of Jack—which had previously been known only from engravings. They can be found in Clare Anderson's article "Oscar Mallitte's Andaman Photographs, 1857–8" (*History Workshop Journal*, 67, 2009).

For the early years of the colonial settlement, Portman's *History of Our Relations with the Andamanese* is an essential source, since it summarizes in detail, or reprints in full, every significant official report on British interactions with the natives. A helpful secondary work is L. P. Mathur's *History of the Andaman and Nicobar Islands: 1756-1966* (Jullundur: Sterling Publishers, 1968), which has the advantages of clarity and concision. Frank P. Myka's *Decline of Indigenous Populations: The Case of the Andaman Islanders* (Jaipur: Rawat Publications, 1993) provides a bleak catalogue of atrocities. In recent years, the Andaman penal colony has drawn considerable attention from historians of imperialism, race, and incarceration. Especially notable: Satadru Sen, *Disciplining Punishment: Colonialism and Convict Society in the Andaman Islands* (Oxford University Press, 2000); Aparna Vaidik, *Imperial Andamans: Colonial Encounter and Island History* (London: Palgrave Macmillan, 2010); Clare Anderson, Madhumita Mazumdar, and Vishvajit Pandya, *New Histories of the Andaman Islands: Landscape, Place and Identity in the Bay of Bengal, 1790–2012*

(Cambridge University Press, 2016); and Clare Anderson, ed., *A Global History of Convicts and Penal Colonies* (London: Bloomsbury, 2018). Anderson's article "Colonization, Kidnap, and Confinement in the Andaman Penal Colony, 1771–1864" (*Journal of Historical Geography*, January 2011) tells the story of the unfortunate Tura and Lokala.

Among the many books that conjure the broader world of the nineteenth-century British Empire, I found David Gilmour's *The British in India: A Social History of the Raj* (New York: Farrar, Straus and Giroux, 2018) especially compelling, as well as Maya Jasanoff's *Edge of Empire: Lives, Culture, and Conquest in the East, 1750–1850* (New York: Knopf, 2005). Jan Morris's sweeping panorama of the Empire at its zenith, *Heaven's Command: An Imperial Progress* (London: Faber and Faber, 1973), while old-fashioned in many respects, offers a startlingly vivid view through the colonizers' eyes, as well as a master class in how a writer can artfully interweave travelogue with historical narrative. Harriet Tytler's memoirs, *An Englishwoman in India* (Oxford University Press, 1986) furnished background information on Colonel R. C. Tytler and his redoubtable spouse. My section on the Rev. Henry Fisher Corbyn (1833–1903) and his unwilling guests at the Andaman Home draws both on documents reprinted in Portman's *History of Our Relations* and on manuscript material in the National Archives of India (Home Department—Judicial).

In tracing the far-flung locations of Andamanese human remains, I have relied on the indefatigable research of George Weber more than twenty years ago. A thought-provoking, well-illustrated essay on the collection and display of Andamanese artifacts is Claire Wintle's "Material Histories: Objects and Imaginings of the Andaman and Nicobar Islands," in

Frank Heidemann and Philipp Zehmisch, eds., *Manifestations of History: Time, Space, and Community in the Andaman Islands* (Delhi: Primus Books, 2016).

For Alfred Russel Wallace's thoughts on the Andamanese and Darwin's response, see Francis Darwin, ed., *More Letters of Charles Darwin, Volume 2* (London: John Murray, 1903).

Chapter 5

Maurice Vidal Portman produced thousands of photographs for his never-completed fifty-volume "monument" to the vanishing Andamanese tribes. Only a handful of images survive that depict the explorer himself, and even in these he is seen only from a distance, an incidental figure, thin and pallid almost to the point of translucency. This ghostly quality persists for me even now, after I have pursued him across several continents. It is astonishing that a person like Portman—the scion of a wealthy and eminent English family, the author of numerous books, and a man who survived well into the twentieth century—has a life story in which large portions remain almost wholly blank. Specifically, we know very little about him before he arrived in the Andamans, at the age of eighteen, or after he left, at the age of thirty-nine. Even Portman's closest surviving relatives—his great-nephews and great-nieces, some of whom were born within a few years of his death—have only a vague memory of older family members occasionally mentioning a certain "Uncle Andaman."

One can catch a brief, tantalizing glimpse of him in an unlikely place: a diary kept by Portman's maternal grandmother in Canada, where he was born in March 1860. His father— the Honourable Maurice Berkeley Portman—was then in the midst of an unsuccessful bid for a career in Ontario politics, having wed a vivacious local heiress, Helen Vidal Harris. Helen never recovered from the difficult childbirth and died within ten days. A local clergyman buried the mother on the same day he christened the son: Maurice Vidal, uniting the names of the dead parent and the living one. (Robin S. Harris and Terry G. Harris, eds., *The Eldon House Diaries: Five Women's Views of the Nineteenth Century* [Toronto: The Champlain Society, 1994].) It was the precarious, ambiguous beginning of a precarious, ambiguous life. Soon, the elder Portman—a womanizer and dilettante—trundled his motherless toddler off to Britain, only to recross the Atlantic within a couple of years to serve briefly as aide-de-camp to a Confederate general.

Then the stage goes dark, and when the lights come back up, a decade and a half have passed. The orphan is now outbound from Britain toward points east, a stripling functionary in Her Majesty's Indian dominions.

Maurice Vidal Portman's service record, held in the India Office papers in the British Library, seemed like it could be a promising source, but turned out to consist of a single page that raised as many questions as it answered. As I note in this chapter, the sixteen-year-old was admitted as a junior officer of the viceroy's state yacht in October 1876, and within a year was listed as "Officer in Charge." How a blue-blooded stripling managed so quickly to attain this position of command remains, like so much else about Portman, a mystery. Equally cryptic is the final entry, a year and a half later, noting that the young officer had been sent on "temporary" service to the Andaman and Nicobar Islands—the posting where he would remain for the rest of his career.

Portman's official activities throughout the next two decades are much better chronicled, in a myriad of other sources. His firsthand accounts in the *History of Our Relations* are fleshed out by regular reports in the *Proceedings of the Superintendent of Port Blair and the Nicobars* (Port Blair: Superintendent's Office Press), which were printed monthly, as well as in the annual *Reports of the Administration of the Andaman & Nicobar Islands* (Calcutta: Home Department Press). In addition to narrative accounts of encounters with the natives (both friendly and otherwise), these include statistical data on the number of inmates at the Andaman Homes, mortality rates and causes of death, etc., as well as valuable context on the broader life of the British settlement. Files from the colonial government's Home Department papers (Judicial), now housed among the India Office archives at the British Library, also include records of various bureaucratic contretemps involving Portman in the 1890s—he seems to have had a singular talent for annoying his immediate superiors—including memoranda describing his anthropological and photographic work.

Portman's handwritten private diary (miscatalogued as *Journal of an unidentified medical officer in the Andaman Islands . . . 1883–1890*) is in the Rare Books division of the British Library, Add MS 70635. In the same repository is another manuscript correctly identified as containing Portman's travel notes from a mission to Little Andaman, Add MS 70634. They were apparently purchased together from an unidentified "F. Edmonds, Esq." in the 1980s; no further provenance is recorded.

Portman appears to have produced at least three sets of albums of his studio photographs and anthropometric data on the native Andamanese. One set, commissioned by the British Museum, remains in that institution, along with numerous boxes of Portman's original glass-plate negatives, which include some images that are not in the albums. (The museum also holds numerous Andamanese artifacts collected by Portman and other nineteenth-century colonizers.) A second set of Portman photographs and data sheets, largely overlapping with the British Museum set, is now in the British Library; it probably came originally from the India Office in London. The richest trove of Portman photographs is also the least accessible: the twenty-six volumes housed in the research library of the Anthropological Survey of India, in Kolkata. It includes many images that do not appear in the two London collections, including dozens taken outside the studio, such as landscape views (some from his expeditions to North Sentinel), scenes of life in Port Blair, and photographs of Portman and other British colonists with native Andamanese. The last volume in the Kolkata collection contains manuscript correspondence, evidently from Portman's own files, between him and various scientists and museum curators in London, as well as other imperial officials. It provides rich insight into the creation of his "complete record in imperishable Platinotype," although it fails to resolve the mystery of his abrupt, permanent departure from the Andamans in January 1900.

For Portman's photographic methods, the best source is his article "Photography for Anthropologists," *Journal of the Anthropological Institute of Great Britain and Ireland*, Vol. 26 (1896). (My first epigraph at the beginning of Chapter Four, taken from that article, has been slightly condensed for clarity.) His article "On the Andaman Islands and the Andamanese," *Journal of the Royal Asiatic Society of Great Britain and Ireland* (October 1881) is a text of the talk that he gave to the Society on the first of his several furlough trips to London, giving impressions of the islanders after just a year or so in the archipelago.

Portman's phrasebook, *A Manual of Andamanese Languages* (London: W. H. Allen & Co., 1887), inadvertently serves as a travel diary of sorts, by providing the dialogue that he considered most useful in interactions between the British colonizers and the natives.

Among the very few secondary works on Portman is the late Satadru Sen's book *Savagery and Colonialism in the Indian Ocean: Power, Pleasure and the Andaman Islanders* (London: Routledge, 2010), which devotes a great deal of attention to Portman's portrayals of the natives in both his writings and photographs. One significant section also appeared in abbreviated form as a journal article, "Savage Bodies, Civilized Pleasures: M. V. Portman and the Andamanese," *American Ethnologist* (May 2009). Although Sen was apparently unaware of the Portman notebooks in the British Library, he drew on a few manuscript sources at the National Archives of India that I have been unable to access, including annual "Reports of the Andaman Home."

Sen worked with the Portman collection at the Anthropological Survey of India in Kolkata and reproduced a dozen or so of the most important images he found there. Distressingly, all of the originals of the Portman photographs that Sen published are now missing, with those pages neatly sliced from the albums in Kolkata and their whereabouts unknown. I am grateful to the editors of *American Ethnologist* for providing me with high-resolution scans.

A detailed summary of Portman's photographic career can be found in "A Biographical Dictionary of 19th Century British Photographers in South and South-East Asia," by John Falconer of the British Library, online at www.luminous-lint.com. It includes lengthy transcriptions from the files on Portman in the India Office records.

The entire second half of Portman's life—between his return from the Andamans in 1900 and his death in 1935—remains shrouded in obscurity. An obituary in the *Times of London* (February 22, 1935), headlined "Mr M.V. Portman—'Father' of Andaman Islanders," refers tantalizingly to "valuable Secret Service work" during World War I and gives a somewhat romantic assessment of Portman's sojourn in the East:

> *Above all men he had the "native touch," that rare, mysterious gift that attracts and makes friends at once with natives; and slowly, through a long period of years, he made his gift prevail—work of extraordinary difficulty, for most of them were as shy as wild animals, and often of extreme danger—he would frequently have to land on their beaches, standing up in an open boat, amid a shower of poisoned arrows. But in course of time he won them by sheer personal magnetism.*

After more than a decade of searching, George Weber was able to find no further sources on Portman's post-Andaman life, including the alleged wartime espionage. I have done little better, apart from a probate record showing that he died leaving property worth just £381—not much, even then, for Lord Portman's grandson.

Every historian ends up making certain discoveries that don't quite fit into the main text but are too good to completely toss out. For me, the biggest and strangest one was the fact that Portman—apparently during his 1881–2 interlude back home in Britain—founded a new order of Freemasonry called the August Order of Light, of which he proclaimed himself "Grand Sacred Hierophant Presiding in the West . . . and Prince of

Kether." The August Order's rituals were said to commingle elements of Hinduism, Jainism, and native Andaman religions that Portman had studied during his travels, with an additional layer of Kabbalistic Judaism that he had acquired from an unnamed rabbi in London. By one account, he claimed to have been "initiated in India in a bath of mercury"; by another, to have acquired the occult mysteries in a chance encounter with an eighteenth-century French mystic, the Comte de Saint Germain, who was one hundred and eighty years old. (See Nemanja Radulovic and Karolina Maria Hess, eds., *Studies on Western Esotericism in Central and Eastern Europe* [Szeged, Hungary: JATE Press, 2019]).

Several Masonic periodicals from the 1880s refer to Portman as having established a lodge among the Andamanese natives. I believe that the photograph on page 148 most likely depicts him surrounded by some of his acolytes, some of whose garb resembles that used by nineteenth-century Freemasons.

Somewhat surprisingly, the August Order of Light still exists today, with half a dozen lodges in England, Australia, India, and Allentown, Pennsylvania.

Chapter 6

For John Chau's life before his final journey, I have drawn on his travel blogs (theruggedtrail.wordpress.com and theout-bound.com/john-chau) and social media accounts (@johnchau on Twitter and @johnachau on Instagram), where he assiduously chronicled his travels and his meditations on topics from scuba diving to Christian messianism. The magazine profiles by Alex Perry and Doug Bock Clark were also useful sources. Chau has also received substantial coverage in articles, blogs, and podcasts by the evangelical groups All Nations, the Gospel Coalition Canada, the Baptist Bible Fellowship International, and Charisma Media.

The tale about surfers at North Sentinel Island, written by longtime surfing journalist John S. Callahan—who claimed to have heard it from the charter boat's captain and verified it with another witness—was published on the Australian website *Swellnet*.

ILLUSTRATIONS

Page 2 The wreck of the *Primrose*, 1981. Photograph by Captain Robert Fore. Copyright © Robert Fore.

Page 9 Columbus's arrival in the New World, October 1492, from *Letter on the Islands Newly Discovered*, by Giuliano Dati, c. 1500. Courtesy of British Library/GRANGER.

Page 10 Detail of the eastern Indian Ocean from a map of the known world by Nicolaus Germanus of Ulm, c. 1482, based on the *Cosmographia* of Claudius Ptolemy (c. 150 A.D.). Courtesy of Wikimedia Commons.

Page 15 Still image from the documentary *Man in Search of Man*, 1974. Copyright © Films Division, Ministry of Information & Broadcasting, Government of India.

Page 16 A Sentinelese bowman aims his weapon at a helicopter, 2004. Photograph by Indian Coast Guard. Courtesy of Agence France-Presse.

Page 34 Boatmen off North Sentinel Island, 1998. Photograph by Adam Goodheart. Copyright © Adam Goodheart.

Page 55 Jarawa boy, South Andaman, c. late 1990s. Photograph by Olivier Blaise. Copyright © Olivier Blaise.

Page 56 T. N. Pandit with Sentinelese, 1991. Courtesy of Triloknath Pandit.

Page 81 Jarawa arrows and basket at Bush Police headquarters, Kadamtala, Middle Andaman, 1998. Photograph by Adam Goodheart. Copyright © Adam Goodheart.

Page 82 "Two adult males demonstrating the shaking of hands when parting," c. 1893. Photograph by Maurice Vidal Portman. Copyright © The Trustees of the British Museum.

Page 87 "Pair of hands demonstrating how to hold an arrow in a bow before shooting." Andaman Islands, c. 1893. Photograph by Maurice Vidal Portman. Copyright © The Trustees of the British Museum.

Page 88 Map detail from *A History of Our Relations with the Andamanese* by Maurice Vidal Portman, 1899. Courtesy of the Library of Congress.

Page 100 "Adult male squatting on a mat," c. 1890. Photograph from Maurice Vidal Portman's unfinished "Record of the Andamanese." Copyright © The Trustees of the British Museum.

Page 113 "Close view of a tattooed chest of a man of the South Andaman group of tribes," Andaman Islands, c. 1894. Photograph by Maurice Vidal Portman. Copyright © The Trustees of the British Museum.

Page 114 The steamer *Pluto* arrives at South Reef Island, December 31, 1857, from *The Andaman Islands; with Notes on Barren Island*, 1859. Courtesy of the Library of Congress.

Page 114 "A girl wearing her sister's skull," c. 1908. Photograph by A. R. Radcliffe-Brown in *The Andaman Islanders*, 1922. From the author's collection.

Page 127 "Adult male drinking from a Nautilus shell," c. 1893. Photograph by Maurice Vidal Portman. Copyright © The Trustees of the British Museum.

Page 128 "Adult male and female sitting on a mat, hugging each other," c. 1893. Photograph by Maurice Vidal Portman. Copyright © The Trustees of the British Museum.

Page 129 "Andamanese group with Mr Homfray, their keeper, photographed at Calcutta," 1865. Photograph by Saché and Westfield. Copyright © British Library Board. All Rights Reserved/ Bridgeman Images.

Page 130 "Adult male sleeping on a mat; another man is squatting behind him; they are wearing head and neck-ornament," 1893. Photograph by Maurice Vidal Portman. Copyright © The Trustees of the British Museum.

Page 131 "Mrs. Ford's Honeymoon group," c. 1895. The two Andamanese men in front are identified as "Moha" and "Daniel." Photograph from Maurice Vidal Portman's private albums. Courtesy of Anthropological Survey of India.

Page 148 Maurice Vidal Portman, Officer in Charge of the Andamanese, surrounded by Andaman Islanders. Photograph from Portman's private albums, c. 1884. Courtesy of Anthropological Survey of India/*American Ethnologist.*

Page 153 "Bullet wood trees, North Sentinel Island," c. 1894. Photograph by Maurice Vidal Portman. Courtesy of Anthropological Survey of India.

Page 154 "Spies hiding in the buttressed trees, North Sentinel Island," c. 1894. Image from an original glass plate negative in the British Museum. Copyright © The Trustees of the British Museum.

Page 167 "Owen," c. 1890. Photograph from Maurice Vidal Portman's private albums. Courtesy of Anthropological Survey of India.

Page 168 Maurice Vidal Portman captioned this photo "Three athletes," c. 1890s. Image from an original glass plate negative in the British Museum. Copyright © The Trustees of the British Museum.

Page 175 "'TIMO,' woman of the 'TA-KEDA' tribe; age about fifty years," c. 1894. Photograph by Maurice Vidal Portman. Copyright © The Trustees of the British Museum.

Page 176 Tracing of the hand and foot of an Andamanese native, c. 1894. Photograph from Maurice Vidal Portman's unfinished "Record of the Andamanese." Courtesy of British Library/ GRANGER.

Page 177 A page from Portman's record of Kaunmu, an Andamanese man, 1894. Courtesy of British Library/GRANGER.

Page 184 Looking for cell service, Little Andaman Island, January 2020. Photograph by Adam Goodheart. Copyright © Adam Goodheart.

Page 190 Maurice Vidal Portman with members of the Onge tribe in front of an indigenous hut, Little Andaman Island, c. 1890s. Courtesy of the National Anthropological Archives, Smithsonian Institution, NAA INV 04422600.

Page 209 Connecting the undersea fiber optic cable at Hut Bay, Little Andaman Island, January 2020. Photograph by Adam Goodheart. Copyright © Adam Goodheart.

Page 210 Indian fishermen on the Andaman Sea, January 2020. Photograph by Adam Goodheart. Copyright © Adam Goodheart.

Page 220 Sunrise, Little Andaman Island, January 2020. Photograph by Adam Goodheart. Copyright © Adam Goodheart.

Page 224 "Jack Andaman," from Adventures and Researches Among the Andaman Islanders, by Frederic J. Mouat, 1863 (image based on an 1858 photograph by Oscar Mallitte). From the author's collection.

ACKNOWLEDGMENTS

No traveler journeys alone—especially when he is working on a book project that spans more than two decades and fifty thousand miles of research trips. I owe enormous thanks to many people who have helped me along the way.

At the top of the list are two longtime dear friends and colleagues without whom this book might not exist: Anne Fadiman and Ted Widmer. As editor of *The American Scholar*, Anne published my original full account of the 1998 journey to North Sentinel Island—even though it was the longest article in the magazine's history. Many years afterward, Ted, as editor at large of Godine, encouraged me to revisit the subject (and the Andamans) by writing this book. Both Anne and Ted are themselves superb writers—and both, in their own ways, intrepid explorers—whose work inspires my own.

Lewis Lapham, editor of *Harper's Magazine*, provided significant support in the earliest phase of my Andaman research. Without this legendary literary man's faith that my voyage to North Sentinel might result in something worth reading, I would probably not have undertaken it.

At Washington College, I am fortunate to be part of a vibrant intellectual community as director of the Starr Center for the Study of the American Experience. Some of my colleagues and students there were surprised at first to hear that—after having published a book on the American Civil War—I was turning my eye toward a distant archipelago. In many ways, however, the two projects explore similar themes of race, place, empire, and the long shadow still cast by the nineteenth century. I owe huge thanks to my Starr Center comrades—especially my estimable comrade-in-chief Pat Nugent, as well as Jada Aristilde, Michael Buckley, Carolyn Brooks, Jasmyn Castro, Amanda Ceruzzi, Erica Fugger, Airlee Ringgold Johnson, JaJuan Johnson, Juliet Kaczmarcyk, Colin Levi, Amber McGinnis, Jason Patterson, Katy Shenk, Kacey Stewart, Molly Streit, and Jean Wortman—as well as to more Washington College faculty, staff, and students than I can name here.

Just weeks after I returned from my second Andaman journey, the Covid-19 pandemic shut down much of the planet. In the midst of that difficult moment, Trevor Potter and Dana Westring offered me a safe, happy, and convivial haven as their unofficial "writer-in-residence." I wrote most of the nineteenth-century section of this book in their beautiful house, and will be forever grateful for their generosity and friendship.

During my travels, I benefited from the kindness of many friends. Particular thanks are due to Julian Ingle for his hospitality and camaraderie in London. Gary Tinterow and Christopher Gardner continue to open new vistas—most memorably during our enchanting sojourn in Rajasthan—and to broaden my sense of the world's possibilities. Robert Worth, Alice Clapman, Zack Worth, and Felix Worth are the best companions that any traveler could hope for.

I dearly wish that Robert Hicks could have read this book. His capacious heart, his convivial spirit, and his boundless passion for storytelling will continue to inspire me. And I cherish the memory of my late friend and former student Seabrooke Carter, a truly adventurous spirit whose journey ended much too soon.

For his insight, kindness, and patience throughout my long

Andamanese explorations, Dr. Triloknath Pandit deserves my warmest thanks. I will be forever grateful to Bala for the help that he gave me in the Andamans, as well as to his family for so warmly welcoming me into their home.

I have benefited from the expert assistance of librarians, curators, and staff at many institutions, including the Library of Congress (especially Abby Yochelson, Wanda Brogman, and Julianna Andrews), the British Museum, the British Library, the National Archives of India, the Indian Museum (Kolkata), the Anthropological Survey of India, the Zonal Anthropological Museum (Port Blair), the Smithsonian Institution, University College London, Washington College's Clifton Miller Library, the DC Public Library, and the Queen Anne's County Public Library.

For inspiration, conversation, and help of many kinds, I thank Samir Acharya; Samir Ahmad; Zubair Ahmed; the late Nelson W. Aldrich; Edward Ball; the Barman family (especially Santu Barman); Louis Bayard; Kitty Bayh and the late Birch Bayh; Sandra Beasley; Sylvain Bellenger and Jean-Loup Champion; John Bethell; Jack Bohrer; Dianne Brace and Robert Lynch; Patrick Callan; Sewell Chan; Manish Chandi; Will Cohen; Claire and Warren Cox; Alexandra Cox and Stuart Sweeney; Patrice DiQuinzio; Dennis Drabelle; Enmei; Captain Robert Fore; Flora Fraser; Charles Francis; Denis Giles; Simon Godwin and Rose Miller; the late Rev. Peter Gomes; Herb, Karen, and David Goodheart; Stephen Greenblatt; Jay Griswold; P. C. Gupta; James Allen Hall; James Hamill; Chris Harris; Eleanor Harvey; Michael Harvey; Wil Haygood; George R. Haynes; Brian Hecht and Doug Gaasterland; Oussama Himani; Richard Holstein; John Jarboe; Maya Jasanoff; the late Karni Singh Jasol; Their Highnesses the Maharaja and Maharani of Jodhpur; Anstice Justin; the

Kanagarathnam family; Dr. Ratan Chandra Kar; Karen Kelsky; Nilanjan Khatua; Stuart Kirsch; Abbie Kowalewski; Lauren Krenzel and Michael Speirs; Anil Kumar; Ashok Kumar; Evan Leary; Andre Robert Lee; Natasha Leland; Morgan Link; Kate Livie and Ben Ford; Jamie Mansbridge; Ratan Mondal; Fernanda Moore; Donald and Ann McColl; Weston Matthews; Jesse Moss; Kiki Munshi; Turi Munthe and Muzia Sforza; the teachers and students of Netaji Nagar Government Middle School (Little Andaman Island); Julie Neithercutt; Andrew Oros and Steven Clemons; Marc Pachter; Vishvajit Pandya; Nick Patterson; Chris Pearn; Aldo Ponterosso; Colonel Michael Portman; the Portman Estate; Evan Quinter; Silka Quintero; David Reich; Brandon Riker; Alvaro Sagasti; Thomas Sanchez and Anthony Shop; Michael Scaldini; Simon Schama; Rob Shapiro; Joshua Wolf Shenk; Scott Shumaker; the late Bakhtawar Singh; Regan Solmo; Janet Sorrentino; the late Vinay Kumar Srivastava; Justin and Olivia Stelter; Jean Stipicevic; Survival International; Aatish Taseer; Vivek Thomas and K Vasantha; Phillip Todd; Richie Torres; Thomas Watson and Andrew Klayman; the late George H.J. Weber; Emerson Wells; and Robert Wilson.

I have relied on the faithful and tireless support of the Wylie Agency through thick and thin, especially from Jin Auh, Andrew Wylie, Jackie Ko, and Abram Scharf. At Godine, I have been fortunate to work with two exceptionally talented, insightful, and patient editors, Joshua Bodwell and George Gibson. I couldn't be more grateful that they have seen this project through to the end.

Evan—I look forward to many adventures to come.

No matter what distance I travel, I carry my family with me. The love that we share for one another sustains me every step of the journey, and it guides me home.

A NOTE ABOUT THE AUTHOR

Adam Goodheart is a historian, travel writer, essayist, and author of the *New York Times* bestseller *1861: The Civil War Awakening*. He lives in Washington, D.C., and on the Eastern Shore of Maryland, where he is director of Washington College's Starr Center for the Study of the American Experience. Goodheart's articles have appeared in *National Geographic, Outside, Smithsonian, The Atlantic,* and *The New York Times Magazine,* among others. He is the recipient of a Public Scholar Award from the National Endowment for the Humanities, as well as a Lowell Thomas Award from the Society of American Travel Writers.

A NOTE ON THE TYPE

The Last Island has been set in Ehrhardt. Released in 1938 by the British branch of the Monotype Corporation, the typeface is a modern adaptation of printing types in the Dutch Baroque tradition. Known for combining a slight degree of condensation with a clean regularity that promotes readability, Ehrhardt is an ideal typeface for books. The digitized version was released in 1991. Walbaum has been used for display.

Design & Composition by Brooke Koven